Mentorship of Special Educators

Mentorship of Special Educators

Jennifer Booker Madigan
Georganne Schroth-Cavataio

CORWIN
A SAGE Company

CORWIN
A SAGE Company

FOR INFORMATION:

Corwin

A SAGE Company

2455 Teller Road

Thousand Oaks, California 91320

(800) 233-9936

Fax: (800) 417-2466

www.corwin.com

SAGE Ltd.

1 Oliver's Yard

55 City Road

London EC1Y 1SP

United Kingdom

SAGE India Pvt. Ltd.

B 1/I 1 Mohan Cooperative Industrial Area

Mathura Road, New Delhi 110 044

India

SAGE Asia-Pacific Pte. Ltd.

33 Pekin Street #02-01

Far East Square

Singapore 048763

Acquisitions Editor: Dan Alpert

Associate Editor: Megan Bedell

Editorial Assistant: Sarah Bartlett

Production Editors: Melanie Birdsall
                    and Veronica
                    Stapleton

Copy Editor: Julie Meiklejohn

Typesetter: C&M Digitals (P) Ltd.

Proofreader: Cheryl Rivard

Indexer: Diggs Publication Services

Cover Designer: Scott Van Atta

Permissions Editor: Karen Ehrmann

Copyright © 2012 by Corwin

Printed in the United States of America

Library of Congress Cataloging-in-Publication Data

Madigan, Jennifer Booker.

Mentorship of special educators / Jennifer Booker Madigan, Georganne Schroth-Cavataio.

p. cm.
Includes bibliographical references and index.

ISBN 978-1-4522-0288-4 (pbk.)

1. Special education teachers—Training of—Handbooks, manuals, etc. 2. Special education—Handbooks, manuals, etc. I. Schroth-Cavataio, Georganne. II. Title.

LC3969.45.M34 2012
371.9—dc23 2011033248

Certified Chain of Custody
Promoting Sustainable Forestry
www.sfiprogram.org
SFI-01268

SFI label applies to text stock

This book is printed on acid-free paper.

11 12 13 14 15 10 9 8 7 6 5 4 3 2 1

Contents

Preface

The intention of this publication is to offer a contemporary, practical, and ready-to-use handbook for professionals who provide support and mentorship to special education teachers. Today's classrooms are very diverse, and the role of special educators is shifting. For these reasons, our book provides a guide to mentoring that uniquely reflects the new landscape in the field of special education. In our preface, we provide a rationale for why this publication is timely and necessary for mentors of today's special educators. In addition, we provide an overview of the topics, activities, and tools in the book.

Rationale

We believe there is a need to distinguish and address the distinctive needs of early-career special education teachers, as well as a need to focus on quality teaching and student achievement within special education for experienced teachers. This also includes general education teachers working in inclusive classrooms. The selected audience for this book includes school district personnel and professional developers for use with mentors who provide support and mentorship to beginning and experienced special educators in the field. The need for support of these special educators is critical. When addressing the current challenges in the field of special education, we must consider the national shortage of special education teachers. Approximately 50% of school districts across the nation have reported barriers in obtaining highly qualified special education teachers (U.S. Department of Education, 2009).

Beginning special education teachers report that they often feel they lack the prerequisite skills for working with their students, particularly students from culturally and linguistically diverse backgrounds. Experienced special education teachers often feel unsupported and overwhelmed by the continuous changes in districts related to No Child Left Behind (NCLB) and the Individuals with Disabilities Education Act (IDEA). Additionally, nationwide alternative programs are being developed as a means for special educators to clear their credentials outside of the university setting; therefore, there is an increased need for pertinent, relevant resources that professional developers and district support providers can refer to and depend on for resources. We believe that this book fills this need by providing up-to-date, research-based information for school districts and professional developers to use with mentors and special educators in a range of settings.

Organization of the Text

Chapter 1, Mentorship of Today's Special Educators, and **Chapter 2, Mentor and Teacher Relationship,** focus on (a) developing relationships between mentors and mentees, (b) identifying expectations and roles on the part of participants, (c) discovering effective methods for mentors to address and support the needs of mentees, and (d) inspiring thoughtful teaching practice by developing a habit of mind for ongoing reflective practice. Included with the chapters are activities to be facilitated by mentors.

Chapter 3, Beginning of School, Scheduling, and Planning Individualized Education Programs: Developing Systems, addresses the fact that organization is a key component of many of the roles special educators perform and focuses on the critical function of mentors to support special educators in their early careers with the establishment of methods, strategies, and systems in order to maintain an upper hand on paperwork, communication, teaching, assessing, and so on. A strong understanding of legal requirements and tools of the trade is provided.

Chapter 4, Supporting Student Learning, concentrates on meaningful instruction and learning for all students. Culturally relevant teaching and differentiation of instruction are presented as avenues leading to student achievement. There is discussion regarding how essential it is for mentors to ask critical questions that move special educators forward in their style of teaching in order to address individual needs. A chart of the Universal Design for Learning is provided.

Chapter 5, Response to Intervention and Positive Behavior Support, is a resource for understanding Response to Intervention (RTI) and the role of special educators in both academic and behavior interventions. The chapter provides a variety of supporting documents for the implementation of RTI interventions and forms to enhance the process of Functional Behavior Assessment as a component of Positive Behavior Supports and academic progress monitoring.

Chapter 6, Culturally Competent Assessment, provides an overview of best practices related to culturally competent assessment, with an emphasis on the use of alternative assessments for culturally and linguistically diverse (CLD) students.

In addition, new regulations from the Individuals with Disabilities Education Improvement Act related to evaluation of students for special education services with specific information related to English Learners is presented. This information is intended for mentor use with special educators to clarify the inherent bias in standardized testing in the assessment of CLD students and to provide tangible options for student evaluation. A reproducible checklist developed by the Education Evaluation Center is a guide for mentor use with a beginning special education teacher.

Chapter 7, Transition, describes transitions that special educators facilitate in all areas of a student's life. Sensitivity to the families served is emphasized and a focus on effective communication with a family-centered approach to transition is presented. Instructional materials and tools for transition are provided to assist students in the development of skills that lead to successful transition experiences.

Chapter 8, Collaboration With Paraprofessionals, offers several activity ideas for the mentor and special educator to engage in to help develop important skills needed for collaboration with paraprofessionals, such as team building, communication, and planning. This chapter provides an overview of some of the issues, challenges, and solutions for meaningful communication and effective collaboration with classroom paraprofessionals.

Chapter 9, Collaboration With Professionals, highlights the essential components for providing the best possible special education plan for a student in the context of professional collaboration. A variety of activities for mentors and special education teachers are provided to guide the planning and implementation of strategies for collaboration with other educational professionals utilizing best practices.

Chapter 10, Communication With Parents, emphasizes the importance of building bridges between the school and home environment. The chapter provides an overview of challenges and solutions for mentors to consider in guiding special education teachers through the process of developing meaningful communication and collaboration with students, families, and the community.

Resource A, Professional Development Case Studies for Mentors, contains case study activities for use in professional development and training for mentors.

Resource B, Teacher Retention and Peer Mentoring: A Model for Success, highlights the features of a special education teacher preparation program that places an emphasis on mentoring in the context of peer-to-peer support.

Resource C, Chapter Tool Kits, accompanies the specific chapters in the book as resources for mentors in their work with teachers to help in explaining, demonstrating, collaborating, facilitating, and providing support with instruction, organization, and planning.

Features of the Text

- *Advance organizers* at the beginning of each chapter to highlight the features of each chapter
- *Activities* in selected chapters to highlight topics and facilitate discussion between the mentor and mentee
- *Case studies* specifically designed for use in professional development and training
- *A model* featuring a special education teacher preparation program with an emphasis on peer mentoring
- *Tool kits* for mentor use with mentees. These tools include the following:

Tools	Brief Description
Tool 2.1. Teacher Information Form	This form is for mentors to record information for each teacher; it provides personal information that can be helpful for the mentor in developing relationships with individual teachers.
Tool 2.2. Meeting Notes Recording Form	This recording form helps to direct conversation during mentor/teacher meetings about what is working and why and what is not working and why, along with next steps and who will do what and when.
Tool 3.1. Caseload List	This is an organizer for mentors to help teachers systematize their caseloads in order to determine schedule of service.

Tools	Brief Description
Tool 3.2. Individualized Education Program Timeline Checklist	This is a graphic organizer that mentors can provide to help teachers keep track of tasks, forms, and important dates for planning Individualized Education Program meetings.
Tool 3.3. Progress Report	This is a resource mentors can provide teachers that solicits general education teachers' input in order to assist special education teachers in writing reports of present levels and progress reports.
Tool 3.4. School Year Individualized Education Program Schedule	Mentors can provide this form to teachers to assist in planning Individualized Education Program meetings for the whole year with school psychologists and other specialists as well as creating an "at-a glance" schedule distinguishing annuals and triennials.
Tool 3.5. Planning Calendar Example	This is an example for mentors to share with teachers to help in organizing all of the components of Individualized Education Program planning: permissions to send home, dates for sending notices of meetings, assessments to administer, and so on.
Tool 3.6. Individualized Education Program Meeting Agenda	This is an outline for mentors to provide to teachers for facilitation of Individualized Education Program meetings with succinct time frames.
Tool 3.7. Individualized Education Program Summary Example	This is a communication tool mentors can provide for teachers that addresses key descriptors of a student, including eligibility statement, strengths, challenges, accommodations, goals, and dates of Individualized Education Program meetings. The summary form is a snapshot that focuses on key elements of an Individualized Education Program for teachers, parents, and others working with the student in the current or next setting the student will transition to.
Tool 3.8. Student Profile	This is designed for mentors in helping teachers to organize information about students on their caseloads for student groupings and monitoring student progress toward goals.
Tool 4.1. Universal Design for Learning Guidelines	This tool is a checklist for mentors and teachers to use while collaborating on lesson design, after conferencing, and for teacher self-reflection to ensure that instruction includes multiple means or representation, action and expression, and engagement. In addition, for each listed item, the online version provides an instant link to the Universal Design for Learning website for additional resources.

(Continued)

(Continued)

Tools	Brief Description
Tool 5.1. Response to Intervention Pyramid of Intervention	This graphic describes the tiers of intervention for a Response to Intervention model for the mentor to use in explaining and ensuring that teachers understand the process and their roles.
Tool 5.2. Twelve Steps for Interventions	This template can be used as the mentor collaborates with teachers and teachers collaborate with colleagues in planning the WHO, WHAT, HOW, and WHEN of interventions for students.
Tool 5.3. Student Success Team Referral	By sharing this form with special education teachers, mentors help them to become familiar with the information general educators supply when referring a student to the Student Success Team. Special education teachers can use this information to familiarize themselves with a student. Mentors and teachers can also use this information to discuss recommendations for the student.
Tool 5.4. Response to Intervention Flowchart	This flowchart clearly identifies the process of Response to Intervention and defines the roles of the team members. Mentors can share with teachers to explain the process and to assist in understanding and planning for next steps.
Tool 5.5. Response to Intervention: Intervention Examples	Mentors can provide these examples of interventions at each of the tier levels in the Response to Intervention model. Teachers can then offer these suggestions to team members and classroom teachers and make use of them personally in their intervention work with students.
Tool 5.6. Student Intervention Summary	This form can be used to summarize student interventions that mentors can share with teachers for data collection and record keeping.
Tool 5.7. Academic/ Behavior Pyramid	Mentors can provide this graphic in helping to explain how behavior interventions follow the same process in a Response to Intervention model.
Tool 5.8. Positive Behavior System Observation Form	Modeling the use of this form by the mentor will assist the special education teacher in observation and data collection for the purpose of behavior intervention. Data collected with this form include antecedent, latency, frequency, duration, intensity, and topography.
Tool 5.9. Student Observation of Behavior	This resource can be provided by mentors for teachers' use in assisting students to reflect on their behavior and helping students make progress toward use of replacement behaviors.

Tools	Brief Description
Tool 5.10. Behavior Progress Monitoring	This form can be used by adults in the student's environment to monitor targeted behavior. This helps with consistency and communication between school and home. Mentors can provide this resource for special education teachers' use.
Tool 7.1. Fifteen Skills for School and Work	This is a transition skill resource for mentors to share with teachers. This form allows students to compare and contrast the skills needed in the classroom with those needed in the workplace. This is a good activity to use when students ask questions such as, "Why do I have to do this math?"
Tool 7.2. Transition Checklist: Middle School to High School	This is a checklist of transition activities for mentors to assist the special education teacher when preparing plans for a student's transition from middle school to high school.
Tool 7.3. Transition Checklist: High School to Graduation	This is a checklist of transition activities for mentors to assist the special education teacher when preparing a student for transition from high school to graduation.
Tool 7.4. Transition Checklist: High School to Postsecondary	This is a checklist of transition activities for mentors to assist the special education teacher when preparing plans for a student's transition from high school to postsecondary life.
Tool 10.1. Teacher Reference Sheet of Family Background	Mentors can help teachers to gather information about the families of the students on their caseloads. This tool is extremely valuable in assisting teachers in communication with families and knowing the culture of their students.

Reference

U.S. Department of Education. (2009). State and Local Implementation of the No Child Left Behind Act, Volume VIII-Teacher Quality Under NCLB: Final Report. Retrieved from www.ed.gov/about/offices/list/opepd/ppss/reports.html

Acknowledgments

What about the children?

—Words of my friend,
Dr. Mary "Peaches" Anderson

I want to thank the women who have inspired me to reach for the stars: My grandmother, Ehrentraut Margaret von Ilberg Oppenheim; my mother, Roberta Carlson; my daughter, Ashley May Madigan; my daughter-in-love, Rebecca Lynn Madigan; and my sunshine, Sierra Skye Madigan. My love and gratitude go out to my father, John Booker; my son, Jerome Madigan; and my grandson, Rocky Madigan, for their support and faith in me through my journey. Finally, I dedicate this work to the powerhouse of my female mentors: Margaret Meyer, Dr. Annabelle Markoff, Dr. Susan Evans, Dr. Elba Maldonado-Colon, Dr. Marsha Lupi, Dr. Peg Hughes, Dr. Mary Male, Dr. Susan Meyers, and Dr. Brenda Townsend-Walker.

—*Jennifer Booker Madigan*

With much gratitude for my mentors: Jennifer, for her inspiration, enthusiasm, confidence, and empowerment; Michelle, for her ongoing support ("You go, girl!") and knowing my heart; Sam, for her wisdom and reassurance; Margaret, for her talents and stories; Marney and Cynthia, for the opportunity to practice my passion with the New Teacher Project; Mimi, for widening my perspective by inviting me, when in our teens, to join her as a volunteer at the United Cerebral Palsy Summer Camp; Rhonda, for listening and encouraging; Mom, for her love and vitality; and most of all, my husband, Pat, for being my soul provider and the love of my life.

—*Georganne Schroth-Cavataio*

Publisher's Acknowledgments

Corwin gratefully acknowledges the contributions of the following reviewers:

Beth Djonne, Staff Development Coordinator
Rialto Unified School District
Rialto, CA

Victoria Duff, Teacher Quality Coordinator
New Jersey Department of Education
Office of Professional Standards
Trenton, NJ

Vita L. Jones, Assistant Professor
Early Childhood Special Education
Department of Special Education, College of Education
California State University, Fullerton
Fullerton, CA

Joy Pearson, Project Facilitator
Teacher Induction, Mentoring, and Development Department
Human Resources Division
Clark County School District
Las Vegas, NV

Ann Marie Taylor, SPED Mentoring Coordinator
SC Center for Educator Recruitment, Retention, & Advancement (CERRA)
Rock Hill, SC

Kim Wachtelhausen, Program Consultant
Teacher Education and Mentoring Program
Connecticut State Department of Education
Wolcott, CT

About the Authors

Jennifer Booker Madigan is an associate professor in the College of Education, Department of Special Education, at San Jose State University. Prior to her position in the College of Education, Dr. Madigan taught for thirteen years throughout the greater San Francisco Bay area, with her experience ranging from kindergarten through twelfth grade in both special and general education settings. As an educator, she had the opportunity to serve students and families from culturally and linguistically diverse backgrounds in a variety of urban and suburban schools. Dr. Madigan's work in schools includes the inclusion of children with special needs in general education settings, and more recently, research on the effects of single-gender special education for female students with mild to moderate disabilities. She has presented this research at state, national, and international conferences. Additionally, Dr. Madigan has received federal and private funding for her work related to gender issues in special education. She has published articles in the journals *Multiple Voices*, *E-Journal for Teaching and Learning in Diverse Settings*, the *National Journal of Urban Education and Practice*, and *Advances in Gender and Education.*

Georganne Schroth-Cavataio is a mentor teacher with the Santa Cruz/Silicon Valley New Teacher Project, lecturer for the Department of Special Education at San Jose State University, and an instructor for Project IMPACT with Santa Cruz County Office of Education, Teacher Development. Prior to her current positions, Ms. Cavataio taught for twenty-five years in both special and general education classrooms. Her educational background includes a master's degree in education from San Jose State University (SJSU) with an emphasis in cross-cultural literacy for an equitable society. Additionally, her educational credentials include Education Specialist, Reading Specialist, and Multiple Subjects. Ms. Cavataio also has a bachelor's of science degree from SJSU in therapeutic recreation with a concentration on serving individuals with physical and behavioral disabilities. Within these many educational capacities, Ms. Cavataio has had opportunities to work with diverse populations ranging in age from preschool through adult. She has published with the education journal *Academic Exchange Quarterly*.

1

Mentorship of Today's Special Educators

I appreciate the support and guidance of my mentor. Being in special education, my mentor has helped me greatly understand the IEP process and helped me understand how to fill out forms, follow timelines, etc. My mentor has helped me develop lessons and activities that support the needs of my students. The most valuable component of the [induction program] is having a mentor who understands the special education field.

—Elementary special education teacher of a multigrade, multilingual, cross-category, self-contained classroom

Chapter 1 Topics, Activities, and Tools

- Mentor's Work
- The Role of the Mentor
- Three Categories of Mentor Assistance
- Activity 1.1. Teacher's Experiences With Mentors

Mentoring conveys preservice learning, experience, and practice to a deeper and more critical level of understanding for special educators. Mentoring facilitates the stages of learning from a conscious incompetence level to a conscious competence level (Revenaugh, 2009). It fosters the special educator's level of understanding from a level of interpretation to and through levels of application, perspective, and empathy. Enhancement of understanding can be accomplished through the mentor's expert modeling and questioning techniques, as well as by directly addressing issues. This influential impact that mentoring has on the teacher's professional development emphasizes the need for skillful mentoring, particularly for special educators working with students in today's schools. In addition to assisting special educators in the rigorous induction process of teaching, assessment, and classroom management, mentoring serves as a bridge for teachers in working with the growing numbers of diverse learners in special education programs across the nation.

The Role of the Mentor With Special Educators

Through reflective questioning, mentors guide special education teachers to resolve implications of their own biases and to focus on student achievement. The instructional, facilitative, and collaborative opportunities, as well as the resources that a mentor is able to provide, help in developing linkage between the teacher's background experiences and that of the students he or she teaches. A watchful eye and ear of a skillful mentor observe and listen for teacher attention, teacher tone, student talk, and student participation. A mentor focuses on instructional strategies and teaching methods that are connected to the experiences and prior knowledge of students and then uses entry points with the teacher to develop thoughtful processes, helping to ensure that learning is equitable for all.

Mentors are an asset in providing sources and support to help teachers develop community resources that aid them in connecting to and learning about the cultures of the school and surrounding community. Because special education teachers rely heavily on parent input as team members for their children's Individual Education Programs (IEPs), credible community resources provide access to information that assists teachers in communicating with families and facilitating family involvement. As teachers plan for conferences, IEP meetings, transition meetings, and ongoing communication, reliable community resources are invaluable.

When special education teachers have made reference to their mentors, descriptors such as the following have been mentioned: *empowering, inspiring, validating, knowledgeable, understanding,* and *supportive.* Ultimately, the mentor's role is to facilitate the attainment of professional teaching standards. The path for each teacher is varied and dependent on copious factors; therefore, the mentor needs to be flexible and fulfill numerous roles. Functions mentors perform include the following:

- Making suggestions
- Advising
- Helping
- Informing
- Consoling
- Listening
- Sharing awareness
- Processing

- Collaborating
- Communicating
- Modeling
- Observing
- Advocating
- Leading
- Facilitating

This work is accomplished in varying formats, resulting in a multifaceted role for the mentor. These roles fall into three general categories: students, curriculum, and professional duties. Figure 1.1 provides examples of situations in the different categories.

Figure 1.1   The Multifaceted Mentor's Role: Students, Curriculum, and Professional Duties

Students	Curriculum	Professional Duties
• Observe student behavior with specific focus and provide teacher with recorded data • Collaboratively analyze student work • Administer tests • Provide a variety of assessment tools • Help design rubrics for behavior and content areas • Help develop student goals based on assessment results	• Collaboratively plan lessons and units of study based on grade level and English Learner (EL) standards • Find and provide content resources • Observe instruction and facilitate reflection and determination of next steps • Provide information on differentiating instruction	• Facilitate communication between teacher and administration, parents, paraprofessionals, and specialists • Facilitate self-assessment and goal setting based on teaching standards • Advocate for teacher with administrators • Help plan and organize for parent communication • Assist in developing system and schedule for communicating and

(Continued)

Figure 1.1 (Continued)

Students	Curriculum	Professional Duties
• Help develop student behavior plans • Help in developing classroom management system • Assist in developing classroom student profile • Help with understanding of characteristics of categories of disabilities • Share ideas for instructional strategies, accommodations, and modifications to meet student needs • Assist in developing a student schedule for mainstreaming into general education classrooms • Help design, organize, and set up classroom	• Model lesson that includes conferencing before and after • Organize classroom visitations to veteran teacher classrooms • Facilitate contacts between teachers at different sites for joint activities • Help prioritize and determine ordering budgeted materials • Brainstorm ways to communicate with general education classroom teachers and develop a communication system	planning with paraprofessional(s) • Participate in events such as transition meetings, IEP meetings, parent conferences, and schoolwide events • Assist in determining school and community resources • Provide organizational tools for organizing and scheduling needs of IEP timelines • Assist in writing IEP reports and completing forms • Brainstorm ways to maximize teacher time and workload by assigning tasks to paraprofessionals and possibly students or parent volunteers • Provide examples of organization, agenda, and handouts for Back-to-School events

Activity 1.1   Teachers' Experiences With Mentors

The following activity can be used to add structure to the conversation between mentors and special educators. This exercise is designed to initiate a discussion with the goal of establishing a meaningful relationship.

Write your responses to the following questions. Be prepared to share your reflections with your mentor at the next meeting.

1. What have been your experiences with mentors?
2. What are the qualities of your mentors that have been the most beneficial to your growth and development?
3. What are the qualities of your mentors that have been the least beneficial to your growth and development?

Effective mentorship relationships should include the following components:

1. Ongoing formal (structured) and informal (naturally occurring) mentorship opportunities

2. Careful screenings of assigned mentors for compatibility with special educators; variables such as background experiences, gender, race, language, and family status should be taken into consideration

Summary

As a mentor listens to the special education teacher's reflections, he or she becomes aware of the individuality of the teacher, understands when the teacher is stuck, and moves toward communication to assist the special educator in viewing his or her practice from a different perspective. In addition to being flexible, mentors need a "repertoire of supports" in order to change hats, moving fluidly from a consulting role to an instructional role, a collaborative role, or a facilitative role (Achinstein & Athanases, 2005). This continuum of support opens doors of opportunities for the mentor to do more than transmit knowledge. In response to our culturally rich and linguistically diverse classrooms, mentors are facilitators of knowledge transformation (Achinstein & Athanases, 2005). This practice can support special educators in the development of their roles as transformative change agents in the culture of the school and community as well as their lives as educators. The teachers grow in their accomplishments and become leaders as their relationships develop, just as the model of the mentor–teacher relationship develops through the mentor's supportive and skillful work.

References

Achinstein, B., & Athanases, S. Z. (2005). Focusing new teachers on diversity and equity: Toward a knowledge base for mentors. *Teaching and Teacher Education, 21,* 843–862.

Revenaugh, K. (2009). Learning how to learn: Step-by-step stages. *Fast Track Tools.* Retrieved August 11, 2011, from http://www.fasttracktools.com/pdf/Learning%20How%20To%20Learn%20Step-by-Step%20Stages.pdf

2

Mentor and Teacher Relationship

Thank you for all you have done in the past and continue to do. I find little [mentor] moments throughout my teaching days where I think back to something you have said or something you have taught me. Thanks!

—Elementary special educator in a Grades 3–5
multilingual, cross-categorical, self-contained classroom

Chapter 2 Topics, Activities, and Tools

- Six Components to Building Supportive Relationships Between Mentors and Special Educators
- Methods for Effectively Mentoring Special Educators Through Setting Expectations, Coaching, and Reflection
- Useful Templates for Organizing Meeting Notes, Teacher Information, and Reflective Teaching Practices
- Activity 2.1. Reflective Inquiry

Mentor relationships and guided reflection about practice greatly contribute to and enhance the development of the beginning special education teacher's autonomy. This becomes more evident as special education teachers, in their second year of teaching, know what to ask for as they approach meetings with their mentors prepared with questions; they are also observed performing teaching tasks with increased confidence. Teachers are able to develop their own voices and then advocate for the voice of every student.

Quality teaching and student achievement result from mentoring excellence that is distinguished not only by a supportive and collaborative relationship built on trust and respect, but by skillful coaching (the heart of effective mentoring). This chapter provides insight and ideas for mentors supporting teachers in finding their voices through relationship development, coaching practices, and teacher self-reflection.

Building the Relationship of Mentor and Special Educator

A mentor's role is multifaceted. Building relationships is the cornerstone of working with special education teachers, and both supportive and collaborative relationships are crucial to teacher success and student achievement. Relationships that are supportive provide guidance and encouragement, helping to create a safe environment where learning takes place. Collaborative relationships are critical to meeting the needs of diverse student populations and provide a more efficient means for reaching student and professional goals (Schroth-Cavataio, 2005).

Lend Emotional Support

Emotional support is something beginning special education teachers are not always able to ask for or receive from school colleagues or someone in an evaluative position. Having a mentor who is in a nonevaluative position helps to develop a safe environment, enabling special education teachers to meet challenges and expand their teaching competence; this in turn leads to individual success and student achievement. The empathy and understanding that a mentor can offer through sharing the same or similar teaching experiences contributes to building a meaningful relationship. Mentors can provide emotional support and instill ownership of success for special education teachers by

- attending Individualized Education Program (IEP) meetings, transition meetings, parent conferences, and department and grade-level meetings along with the special education teacher;

- role-playing specific situations prior to their occurrence;
- coteaching a lesson to help develop confidence in implementing a new strategy;
- pointing out and discussing decisions made by the special education teacher that led to desired results;
- positively contributing to a special education teacher's idea or action by using "and" instead of "but" ("That's a really good idea, *and . . .*");
- trying to anticipate and prepare special education teachers for surprises that occur that do not have "happy endings";
- setting a time limit for venting about challenges in order to be able to coach instead of just putting out fires; and
- leaving a meeting or conversation on a positive note.

Establish a Sense of Teamwork

A sense of teamwork can be beneficial in developing trust and easing the special education teacher's feeling of being overwhelmed, particularly during the survival and disillusionment phases as described by Ellen Moir (1990), executive director of the New Teacher Center. The sense of teamwork is enhanced when the mentor uses language such as *"we* could . . ." instead of *"you* could . . ." when making suggestions and collaboratively developing plans. This helps to alleviate the feeling of isolation for the special educator.

Guarantee Responsiveness and Follow-Through

Other important aspects of developing relationship and trust with the special education teacher are accessibility, responsiveness, and follow-through. It is vital that the mentor is accessible through other means in addition to biweekly personal contact such as e-mail and telephone. Issues with paraprofessionals, principals, students, and students' parents may arise unexpectedly. Having someone to quickly turn to for advice helps the special educator feel safe and not vulnerable. In addition, timely follow-through with support and resources on the mentor's part demonstrates and models thoroughness, respect, and thoughtfulness. It also assists the teacher with next steps, leading to feelings of achievement and success.

Gather Personal Information

Just as it is important for classroom teachers to learn about individual students' strengths, needs, and personal culture, mentors need to learn about each teacher. The special education teacher's personal information can be collected at one of the initial contacts. Mentors may want to create or use a form such as Tool 2.1, the Teacher Information Form provided in Resource C, that includes school site location and contact information, educational background, work experience, and personal information (such as birthday, hobbies, interests, and favorite snacks). Conversations arise around this sharing of personal information, adding to relationship development.

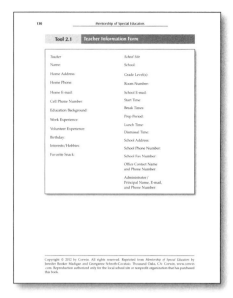

Learn About the School and Surrounding Community

The mentor's role is one of a liaison between the special education teacher and administrator, created and maintained without breaking the bond of confidence and trust developed with the teacher. In order to learn more about the community and professional contexts, mentors can meet with administrators and principals. Mentors are able to learn about the schoolwide focus and events, timelines and deadline schedules (and are then able to help support the teacher to meet those deadlines), and the school's structures, policies, and procedures. Mentors can use these situations to offer or suggest schoolwide professional development opportunities that promote a culture of supportive socialization.

Mentors gain knowledge of the student classroom and community contexts along with the special educator as they collaborate in student assessment, analyze student work, develop lesson plans, and work together to develop student profiles. A mentor can facilitate culturally responsive teaching and assist the special educator in becoming more knowledgeable about the cultures of his or her students and the surrounding community by helping in the research and discovery of their

- ways of knowing (how the cultures in the community acquire information),
- ways of solving problems,
- ways of communicating nonverbally,

- ways of learning,
- ways of dealing with conflict, and
- ways of using symbols (Pratt-Johnson, 2006).

Promote Supportive Socialization

While the mentor assists in the development of culturally relevant teaching that reflects both the teacher's own culture and that of his or her students, the teacher is empowered to have a voice in curriculum and pedagogy that includes high expectations, creates an equitable climate, and addresses diverse learners. Affirmation and promotion of teachers' and students' cultural resources occur with supportive socialization. This is in contrast to "subtractive socialization" in which individual cultural assets are dismissed (Achinstein, Ogawa, Johnson, & Freitas, 2009). Great attention is required to support teachers of color to help promote an increase in a racially and culturally diverse teacher workforce and decrease the teacher–student cultural gap. In addition, mentors can model and facilitate

- structures for a collaborative professional culture,
- professional development related to culture,
- practices that bridge to parent community, and
- access to community resources and knowledge for student and professional learning (Achinstein et al., 2009).

Effective Methods for Addressing and Supporting Needs and Expectations of Special Education Teachers

Identifying Expectations

Expectations are often based on needs as well as established strengths. Knowledge of the special educator's needs and strengths is gathered by the mentor through careful listening during regular meetings and during the mentor's classroom observations of instruction. By having a formative method of regularly recording data such as teacher challenges, concerns, and successes, the mentor is able to determine needs and expectations. (See Resource C, Tool 2.2, for the Meeting Notes Recording Form.) These recorded notes of discussions during recurring meetings with the special educator also provide the mentor with information to use in planning ahead and proactively offering guidance and support. For example, the mentor might prepare questions and prompts in advance to purposefully guide the beginning special education teacher to possible next steps. In addition, the information and data are also available to assist the special education teacher in completing a self-assessment and developing professional goals to address areas of desired growth.

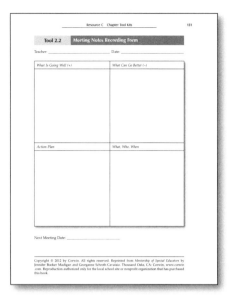

Determining expectations of special education teachers provides a starting point and data for ongoing assessment of results. For example, mentors and beginning special education teachers are able to reflect and verify if expectations have been met and determine what changes or adjustments are needed and/or what new expectations have developed. This helps to provide a guideline or road map, so to speak, for the special education teacher's journey toward developing desired skills.

Special education teachers have expressed expectations of their work with mentors to include matters such as

- help with writing IEPs,
- help with classroom management techniques and strategies,
- regular meeting times with mentors,
- help with lesson planning,
- support in communicating and collaborating with other teachers,
- assistance with developing student assessments and analyzing and evaluating student work,
- assistance with developing and supporting personal and professional goals,
- help in developing student short- and long-term goals,
- help with instructional strategies,
- help in developing organizational systems, and
- emotional support.

As indicated, the expectations are as varied and diverse as individual teachers. In addition, they flex and change with time and experience. Mentors may notice that even though there may be similarities in what special education teachers need and want for support, there is naturally a wide range of skills and expertise amongst special educators. Mentors, therefore, function in what has been described as pacing and leading. Achinstein and Athanases (2005) describe pacing as the process wherein the mentor is listening to the new teacher and coming alongside with empathy. Leading, on the other hand, is holding up higher goals and expectations for the new teacher with guidance in order to promote positive learning experiences.

Coaching

An example of an effective method for addressing and supporting beginning special education teachers' needs was shared by Adria Klein (2007). She suggests applying Pearson and Gallagher's (1983) Gradual Release of Responsibility model of reading comprehension instruction to coaching. Klein explains that literacy language is coaching language used to build up a base of practice by feeding forward rather than autopsying what has already been done. The application of this model implies that both the mentor and special education teacher share responsibility in learning. As a gradual shift takes place, the special education teacher assumes more responsibility for the task. As illustrated in the following diagram (see figure 2.1), the mentor and special education teacher meet for a preobservation conference to collaborate on lesson planning. They will be determining the subroutines necessary not only for student learning, but for the special education teacher's skill development of teaching strategies as well. The mentor may model a portion of the collaborated lesson as the special education teacher observes. Next, they coteach a piece of the lesson, alternating between the mentor having more of a role and the special education teacher taking a larger part. Finally, the special education teacher takes over the lesson independently while the mentor observes. After the lesson, a second conference takes place between the mentor and special education teacher for reflection, assessment of outcomes for both students and teachers, and development of next steps.

This model of an effective continuum of coaching practice can be implemented for a variety of situations in addition to classroom instruction. For instance, the model could be used to role-play in preparation for IEP meetings, parent conferences, principal evaluation meetings, and so on. Increased confidence and effective teaching practice are the results of constructive coaching for the special education teacher.

Through active listening and careful observation, a mentor can determine entry points for instructional, collaborative, or facilitative coaching opportunities. Differentiating based on a special education teacher's skills and needs is key to effectively supporting and guiding the individual toward teaching success and student achievement.

Figure 2.1 Continuum of Coaching Practice

		↔	↔	↔	
Preobservation Conference and Lesson Planning	Coach Models I Do/You Watch	Coach Instructs/ Teacher Assists I Do/You Help	Coach Assists/ Teacher Instructs You Do/ I Help	Teacher Instructs Independently You Do/ I Watch	Postobservation Conference and Reflection
Determine Subroutines	Model	Guide	Practice	Performance/ Application	Assessment

Source: Klein (2007)

Encouraging Ongoing Reflection

Relationships between ideas are built through self-reflection as a teacher unites experiences and brings awareness to thought processes. Reflection is the essence of building connections with others. As teachers share and listen to one another, perspectives are increased and a sense of trust develops (Schroth-Cavataio, 2005).

To address the actuality of our racially diverse schools and realities of racially marginalized groups, teacher reflection needs to reach beyond the scope of their classroom walls to incorporate the political element of their position (Hoffman-Kipp, Artiles, & Lopez-Torres, 2003). Although the reflective process is initiated during preservice and is generally comprised of self-awareness achieved through introspection and based on personal experiences, mentoring for equity is engineered through means such as

- reflective questioning that focuses on students and problems that occur,
- utilizing entry points to develop thoughtful processes, and
- directly addressing issues (Achinstein & Athanases, 2005).

This challenges the teacher to become not only a reflective problem solver but a change agent as well. Therefore, it is a mentor's charge to provide direction for special educators to responsibly and responsively transmit their own learning to others through reflection, inquiry, and other artifacts and practices. A mentor's knowledge and pacing and leading skills are incredibly important for developing this reflective process.

Keeping in mind Vygotsky's (1978) concept of the Zone of Proximal Development, the mentor needs to guide the special education teacher's reflective procedure, scaffolding the process to assist the teacher as he or she gains competence in the use of such practice. As described by Lee (2002b), the mentor

- selects language to reduce any defensiveness the teacher might feel during this discussion,
- works with the teacher to find strategies and resources to redress the curricular imbalance in both content and pedagogy,
- assists in teasing out how low expectations may prevent the teacher from recognizing the potential of students of color, and
- models lessons that provide evidence of what all students are able to do when their prior knowledge is valued and used as an essential element of pedagogy.

Systems of equity outlined by Lee for the mentor and beginning special education teacher to check for and reflect on include the following:

- ☑ Activities for instruction
- ☑ Nature of the learning tasks
- ☑ Student talk
- ☑ Teacher attention
- ☑ Teacher direction
- ☑ Student participation
- ☑ Teacher tone (Lee, 2002a)

Through the mentor's leadership, a special education teacher will become fully competent in reflective practices that incorporate not only curricular and pedagogical concerns, but sociopolitical contexts of teaching as well. Practical formats and artifacts through which this can occur include discussions of successes and challenges encountered during the recurring mentor–teacher meetings when using the Meeting Notes Recording Form and when analyzing student work. In addition, during conferences about classroom observations, the mentor can facilitate the following activity to promote a teacher's reflective inquiry.

Activity 2.1 **Reflective Inquiry**

Present the systems of equity as outlined above at a preobservation conference and have the special education teacher select one area as a priority focus for the mentor to concentrate on during a classroom observation. Discuss specific students and expected outcomes. At the postobservation conference, the mentor shares observation data. The mentor and teacher participate in the cycle of inquiry by studying the outcome (reflection) to determine if goals were met, plan next steps, and implement a new plan.

Summary

The relationship development with mentors, along with their coaching practices, helps the beginning educator transform theory into practice. The guided self-reflection through thoughtful questioning by the mentor helps the teacher to become not only a reflective problem solver, but a change agent as well, resulting in a culturally responsive classroom. Given the complexities of today's culturally diverse schools and realities of racially marginalized groups, special education teachers need to develop skill sets that reach beyond the scope of their classroom walls to incorporate the sociopolitical contexts of their position. In order for teachers to develop the necessary skills to be culturally competent, they need knowledge, understanding, resources, guidance, support, and validation. Effective mentoring for equity is crucial for supporting teachers in this growth process. The role of mentor is an integral component of the solution for addressing issues such as disproportionate academic underachievement, special education referrals, and disciplinary actions that exist for culturally and linguistically diverse students with and at risk for disabilities. This chapter's focus on the components of relationship building, collaboration, and trust as cornerstones for success in mentoring lays the foundation for the important work between mentor and teacher that takes place from the beginning of and throughout the school year.

References

Achinstein, B., & Athanases, S. Z. (2005). Focusing new teachers on diversity and equity: Toward a knowledge base for mentors. *Teaching and Teacher Education, 21,* 843–862.

Achinstein, B., Ogawa, R. T., Johnson, L., & Freitas, C. (2009). Supporting new teachers of color and cultural diversity. *New Teacher Center Research Brief #09-02.* Retrieved from http://www.newteachercenter.org .research_articles.php

Hoffman-Kipp, P., Artiles, A. J., & Lopez-Torres, L. (2003). Beyond reflection: Teacher learning as praxis. *Theory Into Practice, 3,* 258–254. Retrieved from http://findarticles.com/p/articles/mi_m0NQM/is_3_42/ ai_108442653/?tag=content;col1

Klein, A. (2007, February). *Coaching new teachers in literacy classrooms.* Presented at the National New Teacher Symposium, San Jose, California.

Lee, E. (2002a). Checking equity systems. *Reflections, 5*(1), 4–5.

Lee, E. (2002b). Coaching for equity. *Reflections, 5*(1), 1–2, 10.

Moir, E. (1990). Phases of first year teaching. *Newsletter for the California New Teacher Project.* Retrieved from http://www.newteachercenter.org./ articles.php?p=2

Pearson, P. D., & Gallagher, M. C. (1983). The instruction of reading comprehension. *Contemporary Educational Psychology, 8,* 317–344.

Pratt-Johnson, Y. (2006). Communicating cross-culturally: What teachers should know. *The Internet TESL Journal (12)*2. Retrieved from http:// iteslj.org/Articles/Pratt-Johnson-CrossCultural.html

Schroth-Cavataio, G. (2005). Forming relationships: Supportive and collaborative. *Academic Exchange Quarterly, 9*(4), 94–99.

Vygotsky, L. S. (1978). *Mind and society: The development of higher psychological processes.* Cambridge, MA: Harvard University Press.

3

Beginning of School, Scheduling, and Planning Individualized Education Programs

Developing Systems

How can I manage the two triennials next week and the four other signed assessment plans?

—Grades K–5 elementary special education teacher

Chapter 3 Topics, Activities, and Tools

- Five Strategies for Developing Special Educators' Cultural Competencies
- Planning, Scheduling, and Implementing Individualized Education Programs
- Tips, Tools, and Templates for Special Educators' Compliance With the Individuals with Disabilities Education Improvement Act
- Activity 3.1. Individuals with Disabilities Education Improvement Act Regulations and Local Education Agency Individualized Education Program Forms

A mentor needs to be prepared for the many questions asked and concerns expressed (and not expressed) by special education teachers regarding the challenges related to the beginning of a new school year. Challenges often correspond with the many demands made on a teacher's time and the conflicts that ensue. For instance, special educators express difficulties with the number of meetings to schedule and attend, limited time to administer assessments, and the challenge of balancing between those duties and teaching curriculum. Additionally, at the beginning of the school year, many special educators face the challenge of coordinating time with general educators in order to serve students on their caseload. Weekly reflection sessions at the onset of the new school year between the mentor and the teacher should include topics such as organizing schedules and implementing services that address individual goals as well as students' diverse cultures, abilities, needs, and Individual Education Programs (IEPs). Discussions between mentors and teachers provide insights into the need for organizing and managing a system that will assist them in fulfilling their lawful and ethical obligations.

This chapter provides mentors with ideas for support of special educators in starting off the school year. Included is an overview of the Individuals with Disabilities Education Improvement Act (IDEIA) with the specific information that pertains to the legal requirements of an IEP, as well as specific tools for mentors to use with teachers to establish a management system for the IEP process.

Starting the School Year

The days prior to students arriving on campus and the start of school are often daunting for a beginning teacher. Support from the mentor is critical at this point. The mentor should meet with the teacher in the classroom prior to the opening of school to assist with not only the physical aspect of the classroom environment such as classroom furniture placement, work station organizations, and bulletin boards, but to also make certain that the special educator develops systems relevant to culturally responsive pedagogy. The mentor should facilitate the special education teacher's development of cultural competence by scheduling time for both mentor and teacher to learn about the teacher's incoming students, as well as time for reflection on personal understanding of and responses to diversity. Through the mentor's guidance and collaboration, a special education teacher can increase awareness and understanding of how various cultural values can affect student behaviors and how behaviors are interpreted by educators. The teacher will also be able to recognize that expectations placed on students at school can contradict home and community experiences (Friend & Bursuck, 2009). Possibilities for this collaborative effort include

- having the beginning special educator complete a self-assessment on cultural competence (Friend & Bursuck, 2009),
- reviewing student cumulative files and teacher files of current student IEPs,
- discussing skills and responsibilities of the intercultural educator (understanding of diversity, struggle for equity, promoting achievement),
- determining areas to explore about their students and families such as

    o values and beliefs,
    o social customs and mores,
    o rites, rituals, and ceremonies,
    o work and leisure systems,
    o health and medicine,
    o institutional influences,
    o previous educational systems,
    o roles and status regarding gender, social class, age, occupation, educational level,
    o naming practices and forms of address,
    o child-rearing practices,
    o parental involvement,
    o food preferences,
    o culturally influenced learning styles,
    o learning modalities,
    o views on cooperation vs. competition,
    o social function of language,
    o verbal and nonverbal expression,
    o the role of silence,
    o the role and nature of questions,
    o discourse styles, and
    o views on oral vs. written language, and

- determining strategies and resources for learning about students and their families, such as

    o observations,
    o interviews (students, parents, community members),
    o home visits, and
    o the Internet (Diaz-Rico & Weed, 2002).

A mentor needs to take a significant role in assisting special educators in applying what they learn about the students they serve. This essential task of the mentor is crucial in order for teachers to develop their teaching styles, teacher/student interactions, classroom organization, curriculum, parent involvement, and classroom culture that directly relates to students and what they bring into the classroom. This development of knowledge and understanding of their students is also essential for the construction of students' IEPs, particularly goals, objectives, and delivery of services.

Teacher Challenges: Planning, Scheduling, and Implementing

Special educators face the difficult challenges of balancing the high demands of teaching with organizing and monitoring requirements for each student's IEP. More often than not, weekly reflection conversations between mentors and special educators include areas of focus and challenges involving managing IEPs. These experiences regarding job manageability are corroborated by the findings of Billingsley, Carlson, and Klein (2004) and Gersten, Keating, Yovanoff, and Harniss (2001) in their investigations into how working conditions impacted intent to remain in teaching. Billingsley et al. (2004) discovered that the majority of beginning teachers (76.1%) indicated that paperwork and routine duties interfered with their intent to remain in teaching to a moderate or great extent. Gersten et al. (2001), in their interest in identifying alterable aspects of working conditions that could be modified or controlled, found the burden of paperwork to be one of those aspects.

Although it is crucial for mentors to listen and respond to what their teachers are expressing, it's also important to anticipate what those needs may be and to have resources at hand. When mentors are able to discover teachers' needs, they then have opportunities, or entry points, to share their personal systems or to create new ones in a collaborative manner in order to help teachers organize, manage, and alleviate the stress of their work.

Many school districts are now using web-based IEP systems (such as the Special Education Information System, or SEIS). Beginning special education teachers may need training on the system specific to their new school, even if they've had prior teaching experience. A great time-saver for teachers is for the mentor to provide an example of an IEP. Knowing how to order the pages and having an example of content for references are extremely valuable. Because forms differ between regions, it's necessary for mentors to provide their own local forms for their special educators. Some of the web-based IEP systems provide lists of students on a teacher's caseload that indicate data such as the student's birth date, gender, grade level, eligibility, and dates for annuals and triennials. An alternate caseload list is provided (Tool 3.1 in Resource C) that includes additional information such as the content area for goals, the minutes of service, and the general education teacher's name and room number. This caseload list provides easy access and a quick view of students to help the teacher when scheduling services.

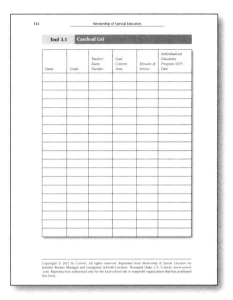

Preparation and Organization

Timelines

Mentors know that juggling teaching and management of a caseload of students' IEPs necessitates a great deal of organization, planning, collaboration, and communication. As previously indicated, several special education teachers find themselves having numerous meetings to organize and schedule all within a short time frame. Not only do the actual meetings need to be planned, but there needs to be a coordination of many people's schedules, administration of student assessments, collection of evidence of student progress, and, of course, the writing of progress reports and drafts of student goals with periodic benchmarks. The following organization tools are included in Resource C to assist mentors in their support of beginning teachers:

- Tool 3.2 is an Individualized Education Program timeline checklist for keeping track of the various forms and notices that are to be sent to different participants as well as determining assessment dates for students.
- Tool 3.3 is a progress report given to general education teachers to complete. The special educator then includes input from the general education teacher as data in the student's present levels report.

- Tool 3.4 is a school year Individualized Education Program schedule. The special educator, school psychologist, administrator, and specialists can collaborate to schedule all IEPs for the entire year at the beginning of the school year.
- Tool 3.5 is a planning calendar example that can be used to input dates of notices to be sent, assessment dates, meeting dates, and so on, helping to prevent conflict between school-wide and classroom events and IEP processes, as well as leaving some wiggle room for unexpected circumstances.

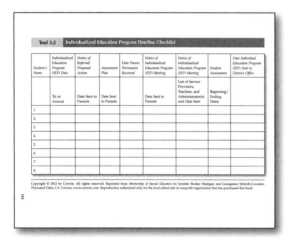

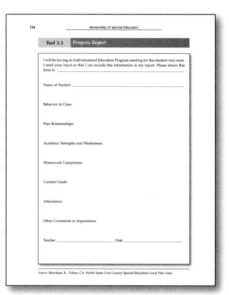

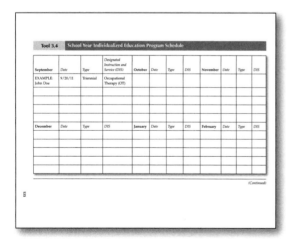

Meeting Facilitation

Agenda and Procedures

Mentors should suggest that special education teachers observe a colleague's IEP meeting prior to facilitating their first meeting. If that is not possible, the mentor and special educator could role-play a meeting to give the teacher a sense of the order of events and responsibilities of the various participants. Tool 3.6, in Resource C, provides an outline of an IEP meeting agenda for mentors to use as a resource.

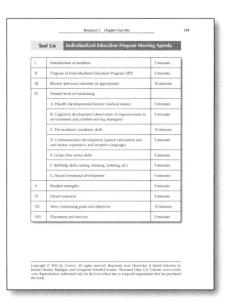

It is very helpful for the mentor to observe the teacher facilitating an IEP meeting in order to coach for any necessary next steps. Following an observation of a special educator's facilitation of an IEP meeting, the mentor can provide data from observation notes regarding specifics of what the teacher was doing and prompt the teacher, through questioning, to focus on his or her next steps for future meetings. Examples of next steps determined by special educators include (1) continue to appropriately contribute to the report and comments of another service provider and (2) maintain a timeline as well as facilitate supportive solutions for the student's challenges by all service providers.

Mentors need to assist special educators with time management so they can send home reports ahead of the meeting dates. Mentors can support their teachers by helping them with scheduling their calendars to include advance completion of reports. Timelines of IEP meetings can be more streamlined if everyone is prepared in advance. Reports sent home in advance of an IEP meeting provide

- an opportunity for parents to get a sense of how their child is performing,
- clarification of additional information that may echo school performance or provide a different perspective, and
- a chance to develop questions to ask at the IEP meeting.

As mentioned previously, many school districts are implementing web-based IEP forms. Several teachers find it more efficient to be able to take the notes of the meeting with the use of a laptop projected for all team members to see. If that is the case, the role of note taker may be rotated among the special education staff while others are sharing their findings. The mentor could volunteer to take the notes in order to model this procedure.

Follow-Up to Meetings

Next Steps

Summaries/Student Profiles

Confusion around the role of each participant in a student's IEP can easily occur for the beginning teacher. In order to ensure that the team's expected follow-through takes place, the mentor should help the teacher create a system for implementing the next steps following IEP meetings. For example, the mentor can suggest that the structured meeting notes from the IEP are used to create a to-do list. That way, even for full inclusion or mainstreamed students who see many other general education teachers and specialists throughout the day, particularly at the secondary level, the special education teacher, as caseload manager, is able to follow through with the recommendations from the IEP.

As special educators discover a need to communicate about the students on their caseload with parents, general education teachers, paraprofessionals, administration, and next year's special education teachers, mentors can help create an IEP summary and a student profile that include essential information from student IEPs. Mentors can explain how these summaries also prove to be useful for the special educators in solidifying information about their students, as well as in planning instruction and assessments for progress toward goals and benchmarks. Tools 3.7 and 3.8, in Resource C, are provided as resources for mentors to help special educators in creating summary and profile pages to meet various needs.

It is important for mentors to ensure that teachers include certain information on the summaries. For example, special educators need to interpret the student's diagnosis/eligibility statement for the teachers and specialists who work with the student. Teachers, parents, and service providers need to know how the disability impacts the student's learning and which strategies to use to

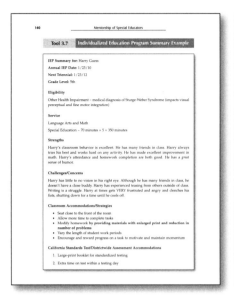

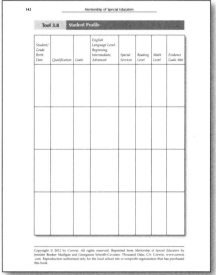

address the disability in the context of the classroom and at home. Special educators frequently request resources from mentors that provide definitions and applications of instructional strategies regarding various processing disorders and attention issues. Resources that mentors can provide include the following:

- The National Center for Learning Disabilities (NCLD) http://www.ncld.org/
- The National Dissemination Center for Children with Disabilities (NICHCY) http://www.nichcy.org/

These websites provide an extensive amount of information for special education teachers' personal use and for sharing with colleagues and parents. For example, NICHCY provides individual fact sheets that describe specific disabilities, including a case history, signs and symptoms, tips for parents, tips for teachers, and additional resources. NCLD provides facts on processing and learning challenges that include skills, difficulties, and strategies to address the difficulties. Mentors and special educators will benefit from creating resources to have on hand that provide classroom strategies to address disability categories and processing disorders. Figure 3.1 is an example of a useful tool mentors can use for easy reference to support the special educators. Teachers can share the strategies with other teachers and parents and include them in the accommodation section of the IEP pages.

Figure 3.1 Instructional Strategies

Strategies Promoting Attention	Strategies Promoting Memory	Strategies Promoting Visual Processing	Strategies Promoting Language Processing
• Give students advance warning before being called on in class. • Provide frequent breaks during the day. • Use colors to draw attention to information, such as highlighters, markers, colored ink when printing, or highlighter tape. • Discuss different ways students in the class monitor the quality of their work such as rereading and checking a list of frequently used words. • Provide students with checklists, written reminders, verbal cues, and so on.	• Use choral-reading strategies so students can both hear and see the print. • Have students answer questions about the text as they read. • Stress self-monitoring of comprehension while reading by using self-questioning strategies. • Teach students to keep track of what they've read by filling in outlines, completing tables, and so on. • Encourage students to highlight or underline as they read and then reread information they have underlined.	• Read written directions aloud. • Use a variety of teaching methods such as direct instruction, small-group instructions, cooperative learning, and working with a partner. • Break assignments and tasks into clear, concise steps. • Give examples of the topic and vocabulary and point out the important details of a picture. • Have a proofreading buddy for notes and essays. • Provide a tape recorder to supplement note taking.	• Give oral directions slowly. • Provide visual representation of information that is delivered verbally. • Draw diagrams on the board; show timelines and flowcharts. • Alert student's attention before expressing key points. • Break down big chunks of information into more manageable pieces. • Paraphrase information.

Legal Requirements

Individuals with Disabilities Education Improvement Act Regulations Pertaining to Individual Education Programs

In addition to providing support and resources to help with organization and planning IEPs, mentors need to ensure that teachers have a clear understanding of the federal regulations guiding the special education process as it relates to the writing and implementation of a student's IEP. For example, the reauthorized Individuals with Disabilities Education Improvement Act (IDEIA) was signed into law on December 3, 2004. The provisions of the act became effective on July 1, 2005, and the final regulations were published on August 14, 2006. The Office of Special Education and Rehabilitative Services (OSERS) in the U.S. Department of Education has prepared a series of documents to support educational professionals in preparing to implement the new requirements. The following information draws from the OSERS publications that address significant changes from preexisting regulations to the final regulatory requirements regarding IEPs, effective August 2006. This information is provided here as a reference for mentors to ascertain understanding on the part of the special education teacher.

Individuals with Disabilities Education Improvement Act Regulations: The Legal Requirements of an Individualized Education Program Effective August 2006

1. Revised general requirements for the content of IEPs

Present Levels of Performance. The term IEP means a written statement for each child with a disability that is developed, reviewed, and revised in a meeting in accordance with 34 CFR 300.320 through 300.324 and must include

  a. A statement of the child's present levels of academic achievement and functional performance and

  b. A statement of measurable annual goals, including academic and functional goals designed to

  - meet the child's needs that result from his or her disability in order to enable the child to be involved in and make progress in the general education curriculum, and
  - meet each of the child's other educational needs that result from the child's disability.

For children with disabilities who take alternate assessments aligned to alternate achievement standards, a description of benchmarks or short-term objectives should include

- A description of
  - o how the child's progress toward meeting the annual goals will be measured, and
  - o when periodic reports on the child's progress toward meeting the annual goals (such as through the use of quarterly or other periodic reports, concurrent with the issuance of report cards) will be provided.

- A statement of the special education and related services and supplementary aids and services, based on peer-reviewed research to the extent practicable, to be provided to the child, or on behalf of the child.
- A statement of any individual appropriate accommodations that are necessary to measure the academic achievement and functional performance of the child on state and district assessments, and if the IEP team determines that the child must take an alternate assessment instead of a particular regular state or district assessment of student achievement, a statement of why the child cannot participate in the regular assessment and why the particular alternate assessment selected is appropriate for the child.

2. Revised requirements for the content of IEPs relating to transition services
   Beginning no later than the first IEP to be in effect when the child turns 16, or younger if determined appropriate by the IEP team, and updated annually thereafter, the IEP must include

   - appropriate measurable postsecondary goals based upon age-appropriate transition assessments related to training, education, employment, and, where appropriate, independent living skills; and
   - the transition services (including courses of study) needed to assist the child in reaching those goals.

3. Clarification of requirements regarding transfer of rights
   Beginning not later than one year before the child reaches the age of majority under state law, the IEP must include a statement that

the child has been informed of the child's rights that will transfer to the child on reaching the age of majority.

4. Identification of the members of the IEP team.
   The public agency must ensure that the IEP team for each child with a disability includes

   - the parents of the child;
   - not less than one regular education teacher of the child (if the child is, or may be, participating in the regular education environment);
   - not less than one special education teacher of the child, or where appropriate, not less than one special education provider of the child;
   - a representative of the public agency (who has certain specific knowledge and qualifications);
   - an individual who can interpret the instructional implications of evaluation results and who may also be one of the other listed members;
   - at the discretion of the parent or the agency, other individuals who have knowledge or special expertise regarding the child, including related services personnel as appropriate; and
   - whenever appropriate, the child with a disability.

   In accordance with 34 CFR 300.321(a)(7), the public agency must invite a child with a disability to attend the child's IEP Team meeting if a purpose of the meeting will be the consideration of the postsecondary goals for the child and the transition services needed to assist the child in reaching those goals.

5. Identification of instances when an IEP team member may not need to attend.

   a. A member of the IEP Team is not required to attend an IEP team meeting in whole or in part if the parent of a child with a disability and the public agency agree in writing that the attendance of the member is not necessary because the member's area of the curriculum or related services is not being modified or discussed in the meeting.

   b. A member of the IEP Team may be excused from attending an IEP team meeting in whole or in part when the meeting involves a modification to or discussion of the member's area of the curriculum or related services if

- the parent, in writing, and the public agency consent to the excusal; and
- the member submits, in writing to the parent and the IEP Team, input into the development of the IEP prior to the meeting.

Changes to the IEP; Individualized Education Program (IEP); Part C Amendments in *IDEIA 2004* Secondary Transition and Statewide and Districtwide Assessments. Documents are available on the IDEIA website at http://IDEA.ed.gov.

Activity 3.1	Individuals with Disabilities Education Improvement Act Regulations and Local Education Agency Individual Education Program Forms

Mentors should plan one session with beginning teachers to go over the specific IDEIA regulations that impact the writing and implementation of student IEPs. The regulatory language can seem overwhelming to a new teacher. By sitting together and reviewing Local Education Agency (LEA) IEP forms, along with the IDEIA regulations, the teacher will be able to see firsthand how the legal guidelines are addressed in the LEA IEP documents.

Summary

When mentors are able to discover needs of the beginning teachers, they then have opportunities, or entry points, to share their personal systems or to create new ones in a collaborative manner in order to help teachers with job manageability. In addition to providing support and resources to help with organization and planning IEPs, mentors need to ensure that teachers have a clear understanding of the federal regulations guiding the special education process as it relates to the writing and implementation of a student's IEP. A strong understanding of legal requirements and tools of the trade are extremely beneficial as teachers confront the challenges of their profession. Since organization is such a key component of many of the roles special educators perform, a critical function of mentors is to support them early on with the establishment of methods, strategies, and systems to maintain an upper hand on paperwork, IEPs, communication, assessment, and planning their instruction. System development must also be relevant to and reflective of culturally responsive pedagogy. Mentors should play a significant role in assisting special educators in applying what they know about the students they serve to each aspect of their teaching in order to ensure student achievement.

References

Billingsley, B., Carlson, E., & Klein, S. (2004). The working conditions and induction support of early career special educators. *Exceptional Children, 70*(3), 333–347.

Diaz-Rico, L. T., & Weed, K. Z. (2002). *The crosscultural, language, and development handbook: A complete K–12 reference guide* (2nd ed.). Boston: Allyn & Bacon.

Friend, M. P., & Bursuck, W. D. (2009). *Including students with special needs: A practical guide for classroom teachers* (5th ed.). Upper Saddle River, NJ: Pearson.

Gersten, R., Keating, T., Yovanoff, P., & Harniss, M. K. (2001). Working in special education: Factors that enhance special educators' intent to stay. *Exceptional Children, 67*(4), 549–567.

4

Supporting Student Learning

How can I make sure I'm serving the needs of my students?

> —Middle school special education teacher of Grades
> 7–8 multilingual, multicultural, cross-category,
> core curriculum classes

Chapter 4 Topics, Activities, and Tools

- Instructional Approaches for Supporting Diverse Learning Communities
- Engaging All Students: Classroom Practices and Standards
- Universal Design for Learning: Guidelines and Checklist for Implementation

As mentors keep student achievement at the forefront of their work with special education teachers, they are able to support teachers in creating environments where learning and student success take place. This is critical in today's classrooms where the composition is hugely diverse and teachers are serving students whose cultures and learning styles vastly differ. Carol Ann Tomlinson (2001) describes these classrooms as being comprised of individuals varying in ways such as

- Levels of emotional and social maturity
- Levels of academic readiness
- Interests
- Learning abilities
- Skills
- Cultural identities
- Physical abilities
- Understanding and background knowledge
- Degrees of experience with native language
- Stresses
- Attentional abilities

In addition, teacher education programs for general and special educators often have not provided adequate training for teachers that promote self-determined communication behaviors and self-regulated decision-making processes to foster successful student–student and student–teacher interactions (Anderson & Webb-Johnson, 1995; Eisner, 2002, cited in Anderson & Madigan, 2005). Teachers and students will benefit from *deliberate instructional approaches* that provide opportunities to acquire knowledge and critical thinking skills (Anderson & Madigan, 2005). This chapter addresses ideas for helping special education teachers design instruction that meets the needs of all students.

Instructional Approaches

Culturally Responsive Teaching

A careful examination of the persistent trend of overidentification of African American and Hispanic male students in special education classes and the lack or poor preparation of the teachers who teach them demonstrate the need to develop high-quality, culturally relevant training opportunities for teachers working with culturally and linguistically diverse (CLD) students (Anderson & Madigan, 2005). *Culturally responsive teaching* as defined by Geneva Gay (2002) is "using the cultural characteristics, perspectives, and experiences of ethnically and linguistically diverse students as conduits for teaching more effectively" (p. 106). Villegas and Lucas (2007) present a framework of culturally responsive teaching for educators to use in developing an effective teaching and learning environment:

1. Get to know your learners and how they construct knowledge. Become cognizant of the learning strengths and modalities represented in your classroom.

2. Be interested in understanding your students' backgrounds and lives. Take time to get to know the families and community.

3. Become socially and culturally aware. If you don't have knowledge about your students' cultural backgrounds, seek out the information.

4. Affirm diversity in and outside of the classroom by demonstrating faith in your students' abilities.

5. Use appropriate instructional strategies for your learners, such as differentiated instruction and the Universal Design for Learning (UDL).

6. Be an advocate for all students in the classroom, on the school campus, and in the community.

Recommendations for Best Practices

A mentor can assist a special education teacher in the formulation of an effective teaching environment by brainstorming ways to incorporate culturally responsive teaching practices into their classrooms. The following suggestions are ideas mentors can share with teachers:

1. In order to develop cultural and cross-cultural competence, teachers can self-assess and reflect on their own cultural experiences while engaging in active learning about the cultures represented in their classrooms (Patton, 2001, cited in Anderson & Madigan, 2005).

2. Teachers can seek out ongoing professional development through school district trainings and attendance at local and national conferences in order to develop culturally responsive instructional and classroom management techniques (Townsend, 2000, cited in Anderson & Madigan, 2005).

3. Teachers can implement classroom activities that promote successful communication learning experiences, effective social communication interactions, and beneficial educational outcomes for students (Anderson & Madigan, 2005).

Instructional practices that lead to beneficial educational outcomes and are well suited for addressing cultural, language, and learning differences include the UDL and differentiated instruction. These methods of strategic instruction are designed to meet the needs of all students by reducing obstacles to learning and providing optimal supports as well as challenges. They are a means to address the varying degrees of readiness, personalities, abilities, and experiences of students who become members of our classroom communities.

Universal Design

The Center for Universal Design (2008) defines universal design as "the design of products and environments to be usable by all people, to the greatest extent possible, without the need for adaptation or specialized design." Three of the various models of universal design that apply to education include the UDL, the Universal Design for Instruction (UDI), and the Universal Instructional Design (UID) (McGuire, Scott, & Shaw, 2006). The UDL is a method for creating curricula that allow all students to acquire knowledge and abilities, as well as an interest in learning. This form of universal design promotes learning and minimizes obstacles to benefiting from the curriculum while encouraging high achievement for all individuals (Center for Applied Special Education Technology, 2009). The UDI is a method of teaching comprised of an anticipatory design as well as inclusive teaching methods that will benefit a wide spectrum of students, including students with disabilities (Scott, McGuire, & Embry, 2002). Similarly, UID is a method that concerns examining the possible needs of all students when creating and carrying out instruction (University of Guelph, n.d.).

Choice, multiple means, and strategic support are critical elements of UDL. Key components include varied teacher presentation (alternatives to lecture style), frequent questions and clarifications, student participation, mixed-ability grouping of students, and demonstration of expectations for student performance. Mentors can provide support for special education teachers to implement the principles of Universal Design during lesson planning, classroom observations, and teacher reflection while keeping in mind the focus on multiple means of

- representation (options for learners to acquire information),
- action and expression (options for learners to demonstrate knowledge), and
- engagement (utilize learners' interests, offer suitable challenges, and increase motivation).

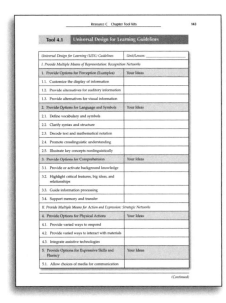

The Center for Applied Special Technology (CAST) makes available an educator's guideline checklist (see Tool 4.1 in Resource C) that provides a guideline for planning instruction.

Differentiated Instruction

Differentiated instruction is comfortable, engaging, and inviting for students. Teachers who differentiate adapt methodology and evidence of learning in response to students' diverse needs while meeting the demands for teacher excellence and addressing issues of equity (Tomlinson, 2001). Teacher design and student choice offer opportunities for struggling learners to become more successful because their way of learning is readily accessible. According to Tomlinson, instruction that is differentiated to meet the needs of individuals is rooted in assessment and is student centered. Differentiated instruction provides multiple approaches to *content* (what the students learn), *process* (how they learn), and *product* (how they demonstrate their understanding). Differentiation of instruction is more qualitative than quantitative, proactive and crafted to encourage substantial growth in all students, and engaging, relevant, and interesting for all students (Tomlinson, 2001). Activities in a differentiated classroom flow between whole-class activities, flexible small groups, individualized activities, and student–teacher conferences. Mentors can assist special education teachers in determining

- the content of instruction based on standards,
- methods and strategies of instruction and processes,
- systems to monitor student progress,
- scaffolding ideas for student success, and
- evidence of student learning.

Embedded in practice that is differentiated is student assessment. The use of strategic assessments directs teacher attention on individual needs and determines instruction. Preassessments are tools that are administered prior to instruction and provide information to the teacher regarding student background, interests, attitudes, learning styles, learning preferences, academic readiness levels, skills, and learning challenges. With the information gathered from preassessments, mentors can assist special education teachers in planning for standards-based instruction, not only the *what*, but also the *how*. Formative assessments are conducted throughout instruction and activities to monitor student progress and help students develop learning goals. Summative assessments are administered following a unit of study. Students are able to demonstrate level of mastery, and teachers report results to parents and administrators.

Figure 4.1 provides examples of various assessments as a resource for mentors and special education teachers. Mentors can support special education teachers in the selection of the appropriate type of assessment to obtain the desired information.

To support special education teachers in creating differentiated classrooms, mentors can help teachers "find their point of readiness" (Tomlinson, 2001, p. 33) and suggest ways to take small steps as a place to begin and then build upon. After determining where the teacher can begin, the mentor can assist the teacher in using a strategy described by Tomlinson (2001) that involves charting a timeline for progress. To begin, choose a few low-prep strategies that will be used consistently throughout the year, along with one other approach

Figure 4.1   Examples of Various Assessments

Preassessments	Formative Assessments	Summative Assessments

• Multiple intelligences surveys
• Home language surveys
• Reading interests surveys
• Writing interests surveys
• Reading assessments
• Skills inventories
• Analyses of student work
• Diagnostic tests
• English Learner data
	• Quizzes
	• Teacher observations
	• Teacher conferences
	• Running records
	• Homework
	• Analyses of student work:
	  ○ first draft of writing task
	  ○ math practice pages
	• Curriculum-based measurements
		• Chapter tests
		• Unit tests
		• Portfolios
		• Culminating projects:
		  ○ models
		  ○ reports
		  ○ demonstrations

that requires more preparation. Next, the teacher adds an additional high-prep approach per unit of instruction or per semester. The following year, special education teachers can perfect approaches from the previous year and add one or two more high- and low-prep approaches. This strategy will help develop a differentiated classroom in a cumulative manner instead of a manner that could be overwhelming and discouraging. If the special education teacher works with different groups of students or different content areas each day, the mentor can suggest beginning differentiating instruction with the group or subject matter the teacher feels is the easiest to work with.

Figure 4.2 provides a few examples of suggestions offered by Tomlinson (2001, p. 34) that involve low-prep activities for beginning slowly and activities that are described as high-prep to add in later.

It is important for the mentor to support the special educator in finding balance as he or she designs a differentiated classroom. This will help the teacher to make progress instead of avoiding progress due to lack of experience or confidence. Along with helping the special education teacher find the pace that is comfortable, mentors may also provide additional support by sharing ideas for the management of the differentiated classroom. Strategies for managing a differentiated classroom offered by Tomlinson (2001) include

1. time-differentiated activities;

2. use of an anchor activity that students do when an assigned task is completed;

3. instructions provided in various ways such as task cards, recorded directions, and key responsible students who share with their group;

Figure 4.2 Low-Prep and High-Prep Differentiation

Low-Prep Differentiation	High-Prep Differentiation
• Choices of books • Homework options • Varied computer programs • Use of reading buddies • Student-centered goal setting • Miniworkshops to reteach or extend skills	• Literature circles • Multiple texts • Stations • Tiered activities and labs • Learning contracts • Choice boards • Multiple-intelligence options

4. a plan for students to get help when the teacher is busy;

5. a plan for students to turn in work; and

6. a plan for students who finish quickly.

Mentors can reassure teachers' feelings of uncertainty about managing a differentiated classroom by pointing out the skills in attending to multiple events within the classroom and abilities in coordinating various roles that they already possess.

Mentors' support of special educators in taking those first steps into differentiated instruction or in perfecting their already established skills will help in the development of a classroom where students' learning differences can be addressed. Differentiated classrooms are both equitable and excellent learning environments for all students.

Engaging and Supporting All Students in Learning

Engaging students in learning entails students taking an active role in their own growth. When teachers involve students in their own process of learning, students are able to develop a sense of pride in what they do. Students are motivated to attain goals they set for themselves and are intrinsically rewarded as they chart their progress toward the desired outcome. Mentors can assist special educators in promoting self-directed, reflective learning for students. Examples include

- student participation in development of IEP and Individual Transition Plan (ITP) goals and periodic review,
- student use of rubrics to make decisions about their own work performance,
- the use of self-advocacy skills and strategies in a variety of settings, and
- defined methods for self-monitoring on-task behavior (San Diego Special Education/BTSA Collaboration, 2001).

It is also vital that special education teachers develop teaching strategies that promote student engagement during classroom instruction. Active ways of engaging students to respond and participate during instruction promote language development and establish a climate of all voices being heard instead of a limited few. Examples of engagement strategies include the following:

- *Think-Pair-Share.* When asked to consider an idea or answer a question, students write their ideas on paper (think). Each student turns to another student nearby and reads or tells his or her own responses (pair, share).
- *Numbered Heads Together.* A five-step cooperative structure used to review basic facts and information. Students number off from one to four. The teacher asks a question. Students consult one another to make sure everyone can answer the question, and then the teacher randomly picks a number from one to four. The students with that number raise their hands, and the teacher randomly chooses one of the groups. The group member with the selected number answers the question. After the student responds, the other teams may agree with thumbs-up or thumbs-down hand signals. The teacher may ask another student to add to the answer if an incomplete response is given.
- *Round Robin.* A cooperative-learning structure in which team members share ideas verbally on a topic. Group members share in order without interruption, comment, discussion, or questions from other members so that everyone has an opportunity to share (*SDAIE Glossary*, n.d.).

State education departments have developed standards for teachers that provide (1) a focus for improving student performance and (2) a means for professional accountability. Teachers are held responsible to professional standards, including those that advance the development of skill areas focusing on student learning such as the use of a variety of instructional strategies and resources to respond to students' diverse needs; the facilitation of learning experiences that promote autonomy, interaction, and choice; the engagement of students in problem solving, critical thinking, and other activities that make subject matter more meaningful; the promotion of self-directed, reflective learning for all students; the connecting of students' prior knowledge, life experience, and interests with learning goals; and the use of assessment results to guide instruction (California Commission on Teacher Credentialing and California Department of Education, 1997). Mentors can enhance special education teachers' professional growth and development toward standards of teaching through the focus on individual student learning. Teachers are able to focus on the learning of individuals through the use of various types of assessments, which were previously mentioned.

Figure 4.3 connects practices of teaching to professional standards and outlines examples of evidence that mentors can look for and special education teachers can plan for regarding engaging all students in learning.

Figure 4.3   Evidence of Strategies and Methods for Engaging Students

Evidence of the following should be visible in the classroom:

- Student interest inventories or surveys
- Student work posted and visible
- Use of visuals, models, brainstorming, and real-life objects and examples
- Presentations and information that connect to student interests and life experiences
- The accessing of prior knowledge by the use of quick writes, Know Want Learned (KWL) charts, questioning strategies, observations, real-world pictures, models, diagrams, brainstorming, journals, graphic organizers, guest speakers, visuals from the students' homes, or personal experiences
- A cultural library in the classroom unique to students' background and interests
- Parent involvement through home inventories, volunteering, notes, and parent conferences
- Opportunities for student preferences by having available a variety of books, tapes, magazines, technology programs, and so on
- The scaffolding of lessons from the concrete to the abstract
- IEPs that reflect realistic goals and objectives
- The review of prior confidential records and the contacting of previous teachers for information
- Additional real-life experiences (such as field trips, career-oriented homework, and basic life skills) (San Diego Special Education/BTSA Collaboration, 2001)

Summary

When the focus for teachers is meaningful instruction and learning for all students, culturally relevant teaching and differentiation of instruction become avenues leading to student achievement. It is essential for mentors to ask critical questions that move special educators forward in their style of teaching in order to address individual needs. Entry points for mentors occur during teacher reflection, during the process of self-assessment and setting professional goals, and during postobservation conferences. It takes time on the mentors' part to analyze teachers' strengths in order to guide and provide direction. As special education teachers build their skill levels, they will be able to attend to the various strengths and needs of students as well as offer more support for colleagues to address the needs of students who may not be responding to universal access in the core curriculum. The special education teachers will also be able to provide the interventions for those students as a result of their focused work on student achievement.

References

Anderson, M., & Madigan, J. C. (2005). Creating culturally responsive classroom environments. *Project LASER: Research to Practice Brief.* Retrieved from http://www.ldonline.org/article/Creating_Culturally_Responsive_Classroom_Environments?theme=print

Anderson, M. G., & Webb-Johnson, G. C. (1995). Cultural contexts, the seriously emotionally disturbed classification and African American learners. In B. Ford, F. Obiakor, & J. Patton (Eds.), *Effective education of African American exceptional learners* (pp. 153–188). Austin, TX: Pro-Ed.

California Commission on Teacher Credentialing and California Department of Education. (1997). *California standards for the teaching profession.* Retrieved from http://www.ctc.ca.gov/reports/cstpreport.pdf

Center for Applied Special Education Technology. (2009). *Universal design for learning.* Retrieved from http://www.cast.org/

Center for Universal Design. (2008). *Principles of universal design.* Retrieved from http://www.design.ncsu.edu/cud/about_ud/udprincipleshtmlformat.html#top

Gay, G. (2002). Preparing for culturally responsive teaching. *Journal of Teacher Education, 53*(2), 106–116.

McGuire, J. M., Scott, S. S., & Shaw, S. F. (2006). Universal design and its applications in educational environments. *Remedial and Special Education, 27*(3), 166–175.

San Diego Special Education/BTSA Collaboration. (2001). *California standards for the teaching profession: A tool to gather evidence for special education teachers.* Retrieved from http://www.btsa.ca.gov/ba/profdev/toolkit/pdf/01-03.PDF

SDAIE Glossary. (n.d.). Retrieved from http://www.suhsd.k12.ca.us/suh/---suhionline/SDAIE/glossary.html

Scott, S., McGuire, J. M., & Embry, P. (2002). *Universal design for instruction fact sheet.* University of Connecticut, Center of Postsecondary Education and Disability. Retrieved from http://www.facultyware.uconn.edu/files/udi2_fact_sheet.pdf

Tomlinson, C. A. (2001). *How to differentiate instruction in mixed ability classrooms* (2nd ed.). Alexandria, VA: Association for Supervision and Curriculum Development.

University of Guelph. (n.d.). *Teaching support services: Universal instructional design at the University of Guelph.* Retrieved from http://www.tss.uoguelph.ca/uid/uidbrief.cfm

Villegas, A. M., & Lucas, T. (2007). The culturally responsive teacher. *Educational Leadership, 64*(6), 28–33.

5

Response to Intervention and Positive Behavior Support

I learned where things are statewide for implementing a three-tier intervention [model] for secondary level at the Council for Exceptional Children conference last week. A [general education] colleague/ coteacher joined me at the conference, which provided her with a lot of information for instruction of special education students.

—Middle school special education teacher for Grades 6–8
multilingual full-inclusion classes and tutorials

Chapter 5 Topics, Activities, and Tools

- Mentoring Practices and the Special Education Teacher's Role in Response to Intervention
- Individuals with Disabilities Education Improvement Act and Response to Intervention
- Implementing Positive Behavior Support
- Tools for Student Success Team, Response to Intervention Implementation, Intervention, Progress Monitoring of Students, and Positive Behavior Support

The role of the special education teacher is changing and continues to be revised as districts implement schoolwide systems in response to students' needs, evidence-based research, and reauthorizations of the Individuals with Disabilities Education Improvement Act (IDEIA). Special educators are faced with the complex task of integrating various evidence-based practices into their pedagogical and assessment procedures. Because each school district creates unique response methods designed to meet the needs of its schools' communities, it is necessary for mentors to be versed in a variety of approaches in order to inform, prepare, and support teachers in their designated roles at their specific sites.

This chapter will present an overview of various models of Response to Intervention (RTI) and Positive Behavior Support (PBS) with practical tools for implementation that mentors can use with special education teachers. Attention will be given to the implementation of RTI with English Learners (ELs).

Mentoring Special Education Teachers in Response to Intervention Implementation

Mentors can assist special education teachers in understanding the RTI and discrepancy models. Figure 5.1 provides an overview of these models for mentor use with teachers.

Figure 5.1   Definitions and the Individuals with Disabilities Education Improvement Act

Response to Intervention (RTI) can be defined as a process by which educators are able to identify students who may possess specific learning disabilities while assisting students who struggle academically within the general education classroom (Murawski & Hughes, 2009). Prior to the introduction of the RTI model, students were identified with learning disabilities using the *discrepancy model* of assessment (Murawski & Hughes, 2009). In RTI, inadequate instruction becomes the area of focus that must be analyzed, while the discrepancy model focuses on the deficits of the student (Batsche, 2006).

The discrepancy model approach differs from RTI mainly in that it requires the student to demonstrate a lack of academic success *prior* to being provided with services, while the RTI model utilizes evidence-based schoolwide instructional strategies that promote the use of intervention at the first sign of nonresponse to traditional classroom instruction (Bradley, Danielson, & Doolittle, 2007). The RTI model makes use of proactive teaching, continuous assessment, data-driven

(Continued)

Figure 5.1 (Continued)

decision making, and comprehensive instruction (Murawski & Hughes, 2009). The RTI model can be beneficial for ELs; however, careful consideration must be given to a student's cultural background and language proficiency in the native language as well as in English in order to ensure appropriate instruction (Esparza-Brown & Doolittle, 2008).

Individuals with Disabilities Education Improvement Act and Response to Intervention

The RTI model is supported by the IDEIA. IDEIA (2004) states:

In making a determination of eligibility under paragraph (4)(A), a child shall not be determined to be a child with a disability if the determinant factor for such determination is (A) lack of appropriate instruction in reading, including in the essential components of reading instruction (as defined in section 1208(3) of the Elementary and Secondary Education Act of 1965); (B) lack of instruction in math; or (C) limited English proficiency; and (A) In general, notwithstanding section 607(b), when determining whether a child has a specific learning disability as defined in section 602, a local educational agency shall not be required to take into consideration whether a child has a severe discrepancy between achievement and intellectual ability in oral expression, listening comprehension, written expression, basic reading skills, reading comprehension, mathematical calculation, or mathematical reasoning; and (B) In determining whether a child has a specific learning disability, a local educational agency may use a process that determines if the child responds to scientific, research-based intervention as a part of the evaluation procedures described in paragraphs (2) and (3).

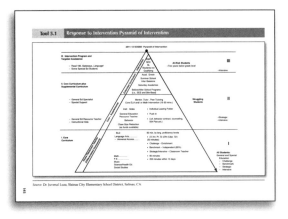

There are various models of RTI that school districts are implementing nationwide. Mentors can provide a broad overview of these models for teachers as a framework for understanding the rationale behind RTI. Figure 5.2 includes a brief description of RTI models and a framework for ensuring success with RTI and ELs. Tool 5.1 in Resource C is a diagram of the RTI pyramid showing an example of a three-tier model.

Figure 5.2   Models of Response to Intervention

Response to Intervention (RTI) models include the three-tier model, the four-tier model, the five-tier model, the six-tier model (Fuchs & Fuchs, 2007), the individual problem-solving model, and the standard protocol model (Berkeley, Bender, Peaster, & Saunders, 2009). In the three-tier model, Tier 1 serves as the tier for primary prevention. This tier is aimed at students in the general education program. Tier 1 is composed of universal screening of all students as well as short-term progress monitoring of students deemed to be "at risk." If a student fails to benefit from Tier 1 instruction, then he or she is moved into Tier 2 instruction. Tier 2 is composed of small-group tutoring in math and/or English, usually in 15- to 20-week intervals. If this level of RTI proves to be unsuccessful, the student is moved into Tier 3 instruction. In Tier 3, a student's educational program is individualized and his or her progress is tracked. In addition, via a multidisciplinary evaluation, both placement and identification of a specific learning disability may occur (Fuchs & Fuchs, 2007). In the four-tier model, five-tier model, and six-tier model, Tiers 1 through 3 serve the same purposes as in the three-tier model; however, additional tiers are added to represent different levels of special education (Fuchs & Fuchs, 2007).

The individual problem-solving model utilizes a research-based intervention designed for a particular student to address that student's educational difficulties. Usually, this model is composed of a recursive four-stage approach: (1) decide what the problems are, (2) devise an intervention, (3) carry out the intervention, and (4) assess the student's success (Berkeley et al., 2009).

The standard protocol model groups students with related problems and provides research-driven interventions that have been standardized and determined to be practical for students with the same type of difficulties for a specified amount of time (Berkeley et al., 2009).

Ensuring Success: Response to Intervention and English Learners

To ensure that RTI does not overlook the unique needs of children from culturally and linguistically diverse backgrounds, Esparza-Brown and Doolittle (2008) propose a framework for RTI to address the specific needs of ELs:

1. A systematic process for examining the specific background variables or ecologies of ELs (such as first- and second-language proficiency, educational history including bilingual models, immigration pattern, socioeconomic status, and culture) that impact academic achievement in a U.S. classroom

2. Examination of the appropriateness of classroom instruction and the classroom context based on knowledge of individual student factors

3. Information gathered through informal and formal assessments

4. Nondiscriminatory interpretation of all assessment data (p. 8)

The authors support the use of universal screening and progress monitoring proposed in the RTI model to allow for comparison of students to similar peers rather than to national norms. Additionally, collaboration among all educators and the creation of instructional models integrating best practices are suggested. Finally, students who are struggling should be indentified early and supported before they lose valuable time in the intervention process (Esparza-Brown & Doolittle, 2008).

Mentors can assist special education teachers in developing a sense of the process for determining students' needs with the aid of Tool 5.2, Twelve Steps for Interventions, located in Resource C. In addition, an example of a student intervention referral form is provided for mentors to utilize to familiarize teachers about the initial steps taken by general education teachers regarding students whose performance is of concern. See Tool 5.3, Student Success Team Referral, in Resource C.

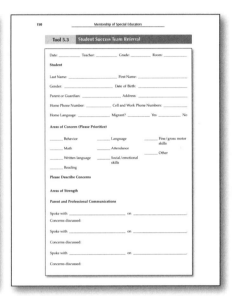

The Special Education Teacher's Role and Procedures in the Intervention Process

Special education services often take on a variety of formats at different schools. The mentor will play a key role in assisting the teacher in defining and implementing his or her role within the school and within the RTI model used by the school. For example, special education services in one school setting may follow a collaborative model in which special education teachers are working as coteachers in general education classrooms throughout the school day. At another site, a push-in model in which special education teachers work with individuals or small groups within the general education classroom may be implemented; a different site might utilize a pull-out model in which students with special needs are included in general education classrooms but receive services apart from the general education setting. In some settings, special education students are placed in a separate self-contained classroom and mainstreamed into general education rooms for a part of their day. As more schools implement RTI systems, roles of special educators may change. One possibility includes the special education teacher working with students recommended for interventions in Tiers 2 and 3. This format would utilize their expertise in a preventative model along with providing special education services for those students who are determined eligible for special education services. An example of a systematic RTI process for mentors to refer and share with teachers (and school sites) is included in Resource C as Tool 5.4.

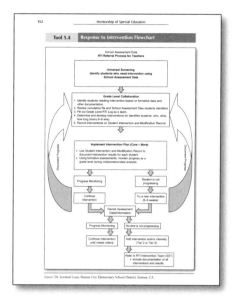

Suggestions for Mentor Use With Special Education Teachers in Response to Intervention Tiers 1, 2, and 3

Tier 1

Within the multitiered model of intervention, special educators serve as resources to general education teachers and grade-level teams regarding student performance throughout instruction at Tier 1. Mentors can support teachers by helping them analyze student work and behavior, finding resources, and developing suggestions for classroom accommodations and interventions.

Tier 2

At this level, special education teachers may provide small-group intervention for students determined to be nonresponsive to classroom instruction. Students already identified or previously determined to receive special education services may be included in this group depending on their individual level of need. The mentor can support the teacher by helping to design

- instructional strategies and lessons that address the student needs,
- assessment tools for determining student performance based on grade-level standards and curriculum, and
- organizational tools to monitor student progress.

Tier 3

Intervention becomes more intensified at this level with instruction taking place in a smaller group size, perhaps even one-on-one, with an increased number of intervention days per week. Special education teachers may be delivering the intensive instruction and the small group could include students already being served in special education, depending on student needs. Tool 5.5 in Resource C offers examples of interventions at the various levels for the mentor's use in explaining the possible teacher roles within RTI tiers.

At this level, special education teachers also will most likely be serving on the Student Success Team (SST) and attending the meetings organized to discuss the strategies and interventions that have been implemented up to this point and develop a plan for next steps. If previous interventions have not demonstrated progress and a continued concern for a student's needs exists, it is possible that a referral for special education assessment would result. A mentor can offer a great deal of support at this level. First of all, depending on the experience of the special educator, it could be very helpful to role-play an SST meeting and discuss the role and type of interaction expected of the teacher. This would also involve the mentor and teacher specifically discussing the student's performance and needs up to this point in order for the special educator to be well-prepared for the meeting. See Tool 5.6, Student Intervention Summary, in Resource C.

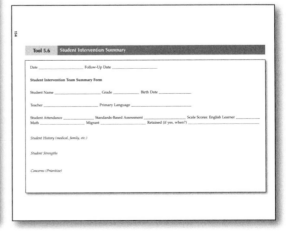

If assessment for special education is determined to be the next step, the mentor can provide support by helping to develop a timeline or calendar (see Chapter 3 Tool Kit) for initiating the process (IEP parent permission signature forms, etc.). Additionally, special education teachers may need support in determining what assessments to administer and how. The mentor may (1) administer part of the assessment while the teacher observes, followed by discussion and/or (2) observe the teacher administering the assessment and then provide feedback. Following the assessments, mentors can assist teachers with report writing, developing recommended student goals, and organizing an IEP meeting. (See Chapter 3 for more information on developing systems for IEPs.)

Positive Behavior Support and Response to Intervention

Positive Behavior Support (PBS) employs the use of educational methodology to augment a student's variety of behavioral and systems change strategies in order to alter the student's environment. The RTI model includes PBS in the tiered approach to intervention. Mentors can serve a range of support roles with special educators in the understanding and implementation of PBS with their students. Figure 5.3 provides an overview of the PBS steps, important considerations for mentors to share with teachers related to the disproportionate representation of minority students with behavioral referrals, and suggestions for mentors when assisting special educators in the PBS process.

Following the analysis of behavior, the mentor can provide support by helping to create the PBS plan, devising replacement skills, and developing consequence strategies. Behavior support plans are generally included in whatever IEP forms the district is using. Other specialists are involved in the plan development, particularly the school psychologist. Provided in Resource C is Tool 5.10, a form for mentors to introduce to teachers that will assist in monitoring and collecting data on the progress of the behavior intervention.

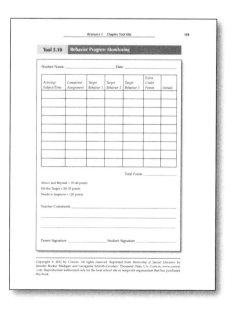

Figure 5.3   Positive Behavior Support Steps, Considerations, and Suggestions for Mentors

The aim of PBS is to improve the student's quality of life as well as reduce his or her difficult behaviors (Carr et al., 2002). There are eight steps in the PBS process:

1. Select a problem behavior of focus.
2. Select a means of measuring and keeping track of the behavior.
3. Invite a team of individuals who have the best interests of the child in mind.
4. Conduct a Functional Behavior Analysis (FBA).
5. Build a hypothesis relating the problematic behavior to the communicative purpose of the behavior.
6. Create the PBS plan.
7. Devise skills to help in replacement of the behavior.
8. Develop consequence strategies. (Sharma, Singh, & Geromette, 2008)

PBS may be carried out at the school level, the classroom level, and the individual level (Bambara, Nonnemacher, & Kern, 2009).

Positive Behavior Support and Disproportionate
Representation of Minority Students

Research suggests that referrals of students for assessment of issues related to behavior by general education classroom teachers are often based on limited understanding of behavior in relationship to cultural influences (Anderson & Madigan, 2005). As Anderson observes, this process occurs when "any behavior causes discomfort for the classroom teacher" (cited in Anderson & Madigan, 2005, p. 3). School districts must reexamine the use of exclusionary discipline policies and consider alternative disciplinary practices if the disproportionate representation of minority students is to be reduced (Drakeford, 2006). Furthermore, culture must be considered when implementing these schoolwide models. Drakeford (2006) proposes the following questions for consideration when addressing issues related to behavior and discipline:

1. Who decides what behaviors are considered appropriate?
2. To what extent is the local community involved?
3. To what extent are teachers and other school personnel knowledgeable about and respectful of local norms and expectations for behavior and sensitive to cultural issues? (p. 8)

Positive Behavior Support and Special Education Teachers

The Response to Intervention model is designed to address student performance, both academically and behaviorially. Just as the tier models were described for academic intervention, the same structure is intended for behavior problems as well. The same process would be implemented as described for addressing academic concerns (see Tool 5.7 in Resource C). In the case of behavior issues, a special education teacher's role may be to perform an FBA for the student exhibiting problematic behavior in the general education classroom. Tool 5.8 provides a useful form that mentors could provide the teachers for use in collecting data and a form for students to use for self-reflection on their behavior (Tool 5.9 in Resource C).

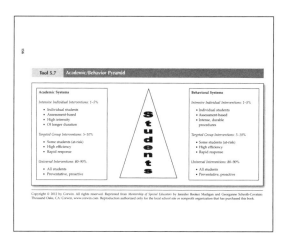

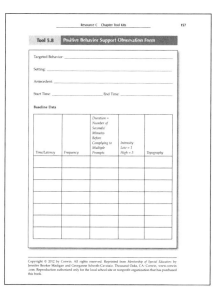

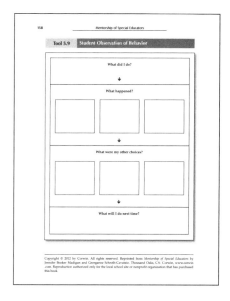

The mentor can help the special education teacher to gain confidence for this role in one or more of the following ways:

1. Conducting an FBA while the special education teacher is teaching, followed by an analysis

2. Teaching while the special education teacher observes and conducts an FBA followed by an analysis with the mentor

3. Acting as a member of the whole SST process

Finally, mentors can encourage teachers to examine and reflect on their own practices and biases related to exclusionary discipline for culturally diverse students by using the guided questions from Figure 5.3.

Summary

The Individuals with Disabilities Education Improvement Act has set into motion new regulations related to the instruction and assessment of students at risk for academic failure. The act states that in considering a child for eligibility of services for a specific learning disability, "scientific, research-based interventions" must be implemented. Response to Intervention is a research-based model based on a tiered system that many districts nationwide have adopted for the purpose of early intervention. The intervention model can have positive outcomes for ELs through the use of universal screening and early intervention, thereby circumventing the possible inappropriate placement of ELs in special education programs. Additionally, the special education teacher's role in campus PBS planning often involves conducting an FBA. The mentor can provide support for the teacher in carrying out the FBA with students with careful consideration of issues related to behavior and culture. This chapter provided a variety of supporting documents to enhance this process. The mentor can assist the teacher in understanding his or her role in the RTI campus process. Special education teachers are often utilized in RTI programs in schools because of their expertise in differentiated instruction and assessment skills.

References

Anderson, M., & Madigan, J. C. (2005). Creating culturally responsive classroom environments. *Project LASER: Research to Practice Brief.* Retrieved http://www.ldonline.org/article/Creating_Culturally_Responsive_Classroom_Environments?theme=print

Batsche, G. M. (2006, January). *Problem-solving and response to intervention: Implications for state and district policies and practices.* PowerPoint presented at the 2006 Council of Administrators of Special Education, Inc., Winter Institute.

Bambara, L. M., Nonnemacher, S., & Kern, L. (2009). Sustaining school-based individualized positive behavior support. *Journal of Positive Behavior Support, 11*(3), 161–177.

Berkeley, S., Bender, W. N., Peaster, L. G., & Saunders, L. (2009). Implementation of response to intervention: A snapshot of progress. *Journal of Learning Disabilities*, 42(1), 85–96.

Bradley, R., Danielson, L., & Doolittle, J. (2007). Responsiveness to intervention: 1997 to 2007. *Teaching Exceptional Children, 30*(5), 8–12.

Carr, E. G., Dunlap, G., Horner, R. H., Koegel, R. L., Turnbull, A. P., Sailor, W., Fox, L. (2002). Positive behavior support: Evolution of an applied science. *Journal of Positive Behavior Interventions*, 4(1), 4–20.

Drakeford, W. (2006). *Racial disproportionality in school disciplinary practices.* Retrieved October 2, 2011, from http://www.nccrest.org/Briefs/School_Discipline_Brief.pdf?v_document_name=school%20discipline%20brief

Esparza-Brown, J., & Doolittle, J. (2008). *A cultural, linguistic, and ecological framework for response to intervention with English language learners.* Retrieved October 2, 2011, from http://www.nccrest.org/publications/briefs.html

Fuchs, L. S., & Fuchs, D. (2007). A model for implementing responsiveness to intervention. *Teaching Exceptional Children*, 39(5), 14–20.

Individuals with Disabilities Education Improvement Act. 20 U.S.C. § 1400 (2004). Retrieved from: http://idea.ed.gov/download/statute.html

Murawski, W. W., & Hughes, C. E. (2009). Response to intervention, collaboration, and co-teaching: A logical combination for successful systemic change. *Preventing School Failure*, 53(4), 267–278.

Sharma, R. N., Singh, S., & Geromette, J. (2008). Positive behavior support strategies for young children with severe disruptive behavior. *Journal of the International Association of Special Education*, 9(1), 117–123.

6

Culturally Competent Assessment

The psychologist helped me determine that my student should be tested in both English and Spanish for his triennial. So I contacted the school district's special education director to request personnel to administer testing in Spanish, and we'll do the testing in English.

—Middle school special education teacher of a Grades 6–8, multilingual, multicultural, cross-category, self-contained core subjects classroom

Chapter 6 Topics, Activities, and Tools

- Best Practices for Ensuring Culturally Competent Assessment
- Mentors' and Teachers' Roles in Evaluation and the Use of Alternative Assessment Procedures
- Checklist for Steps in the Special Education Assessment Process for Culturally and Linguistically Diverse Students
- Activity 6.1. An Analysis of Assessment Through the Lens of Cultural Competence

Assessment is perhaps the most challenging area for special education teachers. The mentor plays a key role in supporting the teacher in the myriad of complex tasks related to the referral, intervention strategies, and assessment of potential learners eligible for special education services. This chapter will provide current best practices and tools for mentors to use with teachers related to culturally competent assessment and an overview of the Individuals with Disabilities Education Improvement Act (IDEIA) regulations related to evaluation of culturally and linguistically diverse (CLD) students.

First Steps for Teachers

Special educators are learning to become observers and information gatherers in the task of determining appropriate evaluation tools for their students. In order to gather pertinent information, various assessment instruments are necessary to measure student progress and achievement. Assessment can be used for a range of purposes including curriculum-based decision making, instructional strategizing, academic achievement for state and federal accountability, and, most frequently for special educators, determining eligibility and placement of students in programs for special education services. All assessments must take into account the student's cultural, linguistic, and ethnic background throughout the process. The standard process of assessment or evaluation for special education students generally includes three main components:

1. Information about the student, including records from school, prior assessment results if available, and significant background and medical information

2. Testing results based on formal assessments, such as the Woodcock-Johnson III, the Brigance Inventory, and the Wechsler Individual Achievement Test (WIAT), and informal assessments, such as behavior checklists, learning style inventories, and curriculum-based measurements

3. Observations of a student in a general education setting (required by IDEIA), used to understand a child in the contexts of school, home, and peer interactions

These standard approaches do not suffice, however, when teachers are working with CLD learners. Alternative assessment procedures are considered to be the most effective way to ensure accurate evaluation of CLD students, given the substantial limitations of standardized test measures. Alternative assessment is informal in nature and emphasizes dynamic and interactive assessment that focuses on the learner's process of problem solving, curriculum-based measurement, and authentic assessment including student work samples and portfolios. Information should describe what a student *can* do rather than what a student *cannot* do. The use of standardized tests to evaluate CLD students for special education services is problematic. Often, the test items are biased or have little relevance to the student's life experiences. Standardized tests can be used informally to provide useful information about a student's strengths and areas of challenge; however, alternative assessment measures are the most effective way to get an accurate picture of the CLD student. The mentor plays a key role in guiding the special educator through the assessment process when evaluating students from CLD backgrounds.

The following key points for ensuring cultural competence in assessment were developed by a team of diverse scholars in a 1998 White Paper. These three key recommendations for best practices have stood the test of time and can be used as a guiding tool for mentors to use with teachers (see Figure 6.1).

Figure 6.1   Best Practices for Ensuring Culturally Competent
Assessment

1. Assessments used for students from diverse cultural and linguistic backgrounds must be valid and reliable. Mentors and teachers can review norm-referenced assessment manuals to examine possible norming bias, content bias, or possible linguistic and cultural biases.

2. Assessment of an English Learner (EL) must be administered in the student's native language. If an assessment is not available, then alternative methods of assessment should be employed, such as curriculum-based measurements in the child's native language and interviews with parents and other professionals who can verify the child's knowledge base in conjunction with observations of the student in academic settings.

3. Informal and authentic assessments, such as writing and language samples, teacher checklists, criterion-referenced tests, homework, and other measurements, should be used to triangulate assessment results in conjunction with information gathered from parents, the student, and other education specialists (Anderson et al., 1998).

Activity 6.1	An Analysis of Assessment Through the Lens of Cultural Competence

The mentor can ask the special education teacher to interview an administrator, school psychologist, or other school personnel involved with special education referral and assessment on the school campus. The following questions may be used to guide the interview:

a. Describe the special education referral process for special education in your school or district.

b. Describe the assessment process for special education eligibility in your school or district.

c. What steps are taken to protect students from biased assessment instruments and practices?

d. How are ELs assessed in your district or school?

The mentor and teacher can discuss the interview information and formulate a plan for ensuring cultural competence for the special education teacher in his or her assessment practices.

Individuals with Disabilities Education Improvement Act: Evaluation and Use of Alternative Assessment Procedures

The purpose of assessment in the context of special education should highlight a student's strengths and challenges with the goal of utilizing the student's strengths to support the areas of difficulty. Special education teachers need training and support when evaluating CLD students. Mentors play an important role in the discussion with teachers of the selection, administration, and use of assessment tools, particularly when the students to be evaluated are ELs. Recent changes in

IDEIA regulations have specifically addressed how evaluation is to be used and the types of evaluation instruments and materials that are to be administered. The following excerpts highlight these changes.

Individuals with Disabilities Education Improvement Act: Changes in Regulations Related to Assessment of Students for Eligibility and Continuance of Special Education Services

1. *Evaluation procedures must be administered in the form that is most likely to yield the most accurate information.* Each public agency must ensure that assessments and other evaluation materials used to assess a child under Part 300 are provided and administered in the child's native language or other mode of communication and in the form most likely to yield accurate information on what the child knows and can do academically, developmentally, and functionally, unless it is clearly not feasible to provide or administer.

2. *Revise procedures for reevaluations.* A public agency must ensure that a reevaluation of each child with a disability is conducted (1) if the public agency determines that the educational or related services needs, including improved academic achievement and functional performance, of the child warrant a reevaluation or (2) if the child's parent or teacher requests a reevaluation. A reevaluation (1) may occur not more than once a year, unless the parent and the public agency agree otherwise and (2) must occur at least once every 3 years, unless the parent and the public agency agree that a reevaluation is unnecessary.

3. *Revise provisions regarding determinant factors.* A child must not be determined to be a child with a disability under Part B if the determinant factor for that determination is (1) lack of appropriate instruction in reading, including the essential components; (2) lack of appropriate instruction in math; or (3) limited English proficiency. (U.S. Department of Education, 2004)

The following checklist (Figure 6.2), developed by the Education Evaluation Center (2007), provides a comprehension framework for considerations and guidelines for mentor use with special educators in the assessment process of CLD students.

Figure 6.2   Steps in the Special Education Assessment Process for Culturally and Linguistically Diverse Students

Step 1: Gather and review existing prereferral information to determine if the referral for special education services is appropriate.

❑ *Assign,* if possible, a case manager who has background in assessing CLD students to be a part of the assessment team to educate the team about acculturation and the second-language acquisition process and culturally responsive instructional guidelines before deciding on assessment procedures. Team members may include parents, bilingual specialists, special education teachers, regular classroom teachers, paraprofessionals, and interpreters.

❑ *Review* existing records and exclusionary factors.

❑ *Decide* whether or not to conduct the assessment based on information reviewed.

❑ *Provide* written parental notification or obtain consent in parents' native language as specified under IDEIA 2004 the first time the student is referred for special education assessment. Review for completeness.

❑ *Encourage* parent involvement throughout all steps of the assessment process by first explaining the reason for referral and the purpose of testing with the help of a bicultural, bilingual interpreter or school professional. Be aware that some CLD parents may view school personnel as teaching authorities and think that it is disrespectful toward teaching staff to express their opinions, especially when they are not in agreement with the school's perspective. Spending time to build a working relationship, while acknowledging and respecting parents' sociocultural background, will be important.

Step 2: Determine the nature and scope of the assessment to address referral questions and comply with laws. According to the ecological and functional assessment model, this is a critical step in the process. If this is the initial assessment for special education eligibility, then a comprehensive assessment should be done.

❑ *Develop* an individualized assessment plan. For many of the components, specific assessment techniques and suggestions will be discussed in the pages that follow. Individualize your assessment approach, since a technique or process used with one CLD student may not be effective with another student due to differences between individual students.

❑ *Conduct* longitudinal observations in multiple contexts to observe the student during the actual learning process.

❑ *Gather* other information as required by law.

❑ *Elicit* parental concerns regarding the assessment as you continue to build a positive, trusting relationship with the parents.

Step 3: Before any assessment activities are begun, be sure that physical causes of school difficulty are ruled out. Conduct an assessment from among the following assessment components:

(Continued)

Figure 6.2 (Continued)

❏ A *hearing screening* should be completed by appropriately trained personnel such as an audiologist or speech and language pathologist with the assistance of an interpreter, if necessary, to rule out hearing as a contributing factor to the learning or behavior difficulties experienced by the student.

❏ A *vision screening* on both far- and near-point tasks should be completed by appropriate school personnel with the assistance of an interpreter, if necessary, to rule out vision as a contributing factor to the learning or behavior difficulties experienced by the student.

❏ Overall *health* or physical status should be addressed.

Once the physical aspects have been assessed, considered, and integrated into the existing information on a given student, the assessment can proceed to the following domains:

Functional Communication Skills

Although CLD students may appear to have Basic Interpersonal Communication Skills (BICS) in some routine settings such as the classroom or playground, this may not be the case in all settings, so it will be important to gather information from a variety of observers such as parents, teachers, support staff, and so on. Remember, it takes two to three years in the dominant culture to acquire BICS.

❏ Assess the level of functional communication (BICS).

Language

❏ Assess the level of language proficiency using Cognitive Academic Linguistic Proficiency (CALP).

❏ Determine the level of acculturation.

Additional Tools and Suggestions

❏ Parent interview/questionnaires

❏ Direct observation in a variety of settings

    o Structured setting (such as a classroom), and

    o Unstructured setting (such as the playground, the lunchroom, or a physical education class)

❏ Behavioral sampling

❏ Portfolio assessment of work samples

❏ Language, writing, and narrative sampling in all languages

❏ Structured probe assessment

❏ Standardized and norm-referenced tests (only if normative data include the population in question)

❏ Criterion-referenced tests

❏ Dynamic assessment

❏ Cloze techniques

❏ *Determine* student eligibility by referring to local school district guidelines. In addition, in view of the special needs of the CLD population, the following considerations are offered:

    o The current trend of identifying learning disabilities utilizing a discrepancy model based on standardized test score discrepancies has been criticized as lacking validity in determining special education eligibility. Exclusionary factors relevant to CLD students further the problematic use of standardized measures for this population and other multiple and mixed methods of eligibility determination are likely necessary.

Do

- Consider a student's language usage opportunities and exposure in the home, school, and community settings as well as his or her language proficiency before determining the language used for further testing.
- Administer a standardized test if the test was normed in the population the student belongs to and test items are within his or her realm of experience.
- Correlate standardized and informal test results.
- Use only well-trained and educated interpreters.
- Use standardized tests dynamically (test, teach, and retest) and report results in narrative form with no scores.
- Use multiple measures and contexts to assess.

Don't

- Translate standardized tests.
- Modify a standardized test without documenting modifications and then discussing performance rather than reporting scores.
- Report test scores if standardization procedures were violated.
- Use tests that measure factual information and learned content.
- Make eligibility decisions based on a single test. (Education Evaluation Center, 2007)

Summary

This chapter provided an overview of best practices related to culturally competent assessment, with an emphasis on the use of alternative assessments for CLD students. Additionally, new regulations from IDEIA related to evaluation of students for special education services with specific information related to ELs were presented. This information is intended for mentor use with special educators to clarify the inherent bias in standardized testing in the assessment of CLD students and to provide tangible options for student evaluation. A reproducible checklist developed by the Education Evaluation Center is a guide for mentor use with special education teachers. Accurately derived information is essential for teachers to be able to attend to the needs of students, design instruction, and plan activities that are appropriate for addressing grade-level standards and students' transitions throughout their academic career.

References

Anderson, M., Beard, K., Delgado, B., Kea, C., Raymond, E., Singh, N., . . . Webb-Johnson, G. (1998). *Working with culturally and linguistically diverse children, youth, and their families: Promising practices in assessment, instruction, and personnel preparation* [White paper]. Reston, VA: Council for Children With Behavioral Disorders.

Education Evaluation Center. (2007). *Assessment process for culturally and linguistically diverse Students: Guidelines and resources.* The Teaching Research Institute: Western Oregon University.

U.S. Department of Education. (2004). *IDEA regulation: Changes in initial evaluation and reevaluation.* Retrieved from http://idea.ed.gov/explore/view/p/%2Croot%2Cdynamic%2CTopicalBrief%2C4%2C

7

Transition

Knowledge [about the preschool program] would have been bene-ficial at the beginning of the year to help with [the student's] transition.

—Elementary teacher of a Grades K–5 self-contained
cross-categorical special education classroom

Chapter 7 Topics, Activities, and Tools

- Legislation and Current Issues in the Transition of Students in Special Education
- In School, Through School, and Beyond School: Instructional Strategies for Transition
- Activity 7.1. Visitation and Observation of the Program Prior To and/or Following Students' Current Special Education Program
- Activity 7.2. Create Family Assessment Portfolios
- Tools for Transition Skills and Checklists

Mentors can guide special educators in legal requirements and best practices to instruct and prepare students, beginning at an early age, for the transitions they encounter on a daily basis. Best practices need to include ongoing communication with families. This chapter offers suggestions for mentors as they assist special education teachers in creating, planning, organizing, instructing, and facilitating activities to prepare students for a variety of transitions. Information that addresses challenges regarding culturally and linguistically diverse (CLD) families is included for mentors to use as a reference and to share with educators in preparation for transitions.

Individuals with Disabilities Education Improvement Act and Transition

An important aspect of the transition process is individualization for students and their families. Individualizing involves basing the course of action not only on needs but also on cultural perspectives. Although transition is addressed in the Individuals with Disabilities Education Improvement Act (IDEIA) between birth and 3 years of age through the Individualized Family Service Plan (IFSP) and through the Individualized Transition Plan (ITP) when a student reaches the age of 16, it is important for mentors to emphasize to special education teachers that students and their families are experiencing transition as an ongoing process. Figure 7.1 highlights the two significant formal transitions that occur under IDEIA between birth and 3 years and again at age 16.

Figure 7.1   Individuals with Disabilities Education Improvement Act and Transition

Guidelines for the Individualized Family Service Plan Under Part C of Individuals with Disabilities Education Improvement Act: Birth to Age 3

Part C of IDEIA is a discretionary program that awards grants to states to provide early intervention services to the families of infants and toddlers (birth to age 3) who have disabilities including developmental delays. In order for a state to participate in the program, it must ensure that early intervention will be available to every eligible child and his or her family. Each state defines developmental delay for itself and may choose to serve infants and toddlers who are at risk of developing disabilities. Unlike in Part B, services are not necessarily free. Agencies are allowed to charge for services on a sliding scale. Currently, all states participate in Part C.

*Individuals with Disabilities Education Improvement
Act Part B: Transition at Age 16*

Beginning no later than the first Individualized Education Program (IEP) to be in effect when the child turns 16, or younger if determined appropriate by the IEP team, and updated annually thereafter, the IEP must include

- appropriate measurable postsecondary goals based upon age-appropriate transition assessments related to training, education, employment, and, where appropriate, independent living skills; and
- the transition services (including courses of study) needed to assist the child in reaching those goals. (IDEIA, 2004)

Transition Issues

Dr. Gary Greene (2009) emphasizes unique challenges faced by CLD families and describes the process of transition into, through, and beyond school for youth with disabilities and their families as complex, stressful, and challenging. All of these transition periods represent more challenges to CLD families due to their minority status, insensitivities on the part of professionals toward cultural group differences, value differences, and contextual barriers (Greene, 2009). Greene outlines these major transitions across a lifespan (see Figure 7.2).

Figure 7.2 Transitions

Into School

Members of a family encounter many changes and find themselves having to make several adjustments due to regulations that change between their Individual Family Service Plan and their child's Individualized Education Program that address the Individuals with Disabilities Education Improvement Act legal requirements. They discover that services are more student centered and less family centered, resulting in a sense of isolation. Families often experience feelings of fear and anxiety around their children's attendance at school where concerns about their children's educational needs manifest (Greene, 2009).

(Continued)

Figure 7.2 (Continued)

Through School

As students make the transition from elementary school to middle school, they face challenges regarding the structure of the new system that includes multiple classes and teachers. There are more pressures from peer groups and challenges in developing appropriate social skills. Academics are more complex and demanding.

The move from middle school to high school brings opportunities and challenges involving the selection of a course of study. The focus is on planning for transition and investigating available programs and services. Frequently, issues of the culturally and linguistically diverse adolescent are not addressed and services or support are unresponsive to their needs (Greene, 2009).

Beyond School

Determining appropriate options for the next steps after high school can be overwhelming, particularly if there are language barriers and major differences in family values between those seeking services and those helping to plan and facilitate services. Sometimes the emphasis on independence is unwelcomed by cultures that value interdependence. Considerations for families of young adults with disabilities include the following:

- Postsecondary education and training options
- Community participation and competence
- Employment
- Daily living skills
- Functional vocational evaluation
- Transition service agencies and resources (Greene, 2009)

An examination of culturally based variations in attitudes and beliefs about transition was conducted by Rueda, Monzo, Shapiro, Gomez, and Blacher (2005). Participants in their study included 16 Latina mothers of young adults with disabilities. The researchers found that "the overarching theme was a view of transition as home-centered, sheltered adaptation as opposed to a model emphasizing independent productivity" (p. 401). The primary identified themes, which appear to be at odds with the service delivery system, are shown in Figure 7.3.

In addition to studying culturally based variations regarding transition, Hogansen, Powers, Geenen, Gil-Kashiwabara, and Powers (2008) studied the influence of gender on the transition goals and experiences of female students with disabilities. They found that females have unique experiences in regards to the types of transition goals established for them, determined by the factors shown in Figure 7.4.

Figure 7.3   Variations in Attitudes and Beliefs About Transition

- Basic life skills and social adaptation (concern for continued development of basic life skills and ways to handle relationships with the opposite sex)
- The importance of family and home over individualism and independence
- The importance of the mother's role and expertise in decision making
- Access to information (desire for more information)
- Dangers of the outside world (perceived lack of adequate supervision in work placements and possibility of discrimination) (Rueda et al., 2005)

Figure 7.4   Factors Affecting Transition Goals for Female Students

- Self-perception (the fear of other people's negative perceptions of their disabilities)
- Mentors (lack of skill and career mentors)
- Peers (friends provide support; parents worry that transition goals might be influenced by male relationships)
- Family (parents concerned with safety)
- Exposure to opportunities (concern about gender bias in school-based work experience programs)

Mentors can assist special educators by helping to create awareness and develop systems that address needs related to the student's cultural context and gender in order to provide transition supports that are meaningful and applicable (Hogansen et al., 2008).

Planning for Transition

Mentors can facilitate, organize, and provide support for special educators in the transition process with their students and families. The following ideas are offered as an outline of tasks, activities, and opportunities for mentors to address with special education teachers regarding transition planning and processes.

Opportunities for mentors to assist teachers in developing appropriate transition supports for students occur during collaboration and reflection but could also include visitations to students' previous special education program or the program students will be transitioning into the following year. Visitations provide a wealth of information about students' prior experiences and information about what's to come for the students that special education teachers can build upon, better equipping them to help students plan for and make the transitions.

Activity 7.1	Visitation and Observation of the Program Prior To and/or Following Students' Current Special Education Program

Mentors can plan, organize, schedule, and facilitate visitations for special education teachers to

- Visit the programs for students that lead up to or follow the grade level with which the special education teacher works (for example, if a teacher works with elementary grade levels, have him or her visit the preschool program and the middle school program).
- Observe a colleague's transition meeting for those programs.

Developing Processes

In order to address obstacles faced by CLD families in the service delivery system regarding transition, mentors supporting special education teachers in developing processes could include means for the following:

- Getting to know the student's family really well
- Helping parents know what to do at a transition meeting
- Holding transition meetings in the family's home or with a translator from the community, such as the family's pastor
- Explaining IDEIA and how it defines transition
- Developing community mentor groups composed of families who have gone through the system (Greene, 2009)
- Creating self-esteem development activities
- Providing parents with information on an ongoing basis
- Establishing relationships that enable professionals, families, and students to earnestly work together
- Including students in transition planning
- Asking families and students about their gender expectations, cultural traditions, and family backgrounds
- Creating job shadowing and training opportunities, informational interviews, and networking (Hogansen et al., 2008)

In addition, having family members work together to create a family assessment portfolio can promote collaboration between school and home by involving the family in the assessment process, increasing opportunities for family members to share important information with the school about their child, and familiarizing school personnel with the child's likes, dislikes, strengths, and needs (Thompson, Meadan, Fansler, Alber, & Balogh, 2007). Mentors can facilitate the following activity for teachers to promote with families, particularly at the early education level.

Activity 7.2	Create Family Assessment Portfolios

Create a student scrapbook as an example for parents to make for their child that includes sections such as these:

- All About Me—Introduce the child with personal information
- Meet My Family and Friends—Tell about the family, extended family, friends, and pets
- Learn About My Disability—Include practical information, such as a list or description of accommodations and modifications a student will need in the classroom for his or her disability
- Look What I Can Do!—Share an overview of the child's current level of performance
- Things to Remember—Create a summary of information for teachers to remember
- Words From People Who Know Me—Present information about the child from the perspective of loving family and friends (Thompson et al., 2007)

Planning and Implementing

The mentor can help the special education teacher pull together all the information and use it to address individual and family concerns through instructive, collaborative, and facilitative coaching practices that include

- familiarizing the special educator with the IDEIA requirements around transition;
- planning and organizing transition meetings;

- addressing issues such as attendees, translators, location, IEP forms, and the compilation of information to share about individual students; and
- investigating student-led IEPs and helping to determine a small first (or next) step.

By working together with special educators, mentors can help ensure that student and family needs are addressed.

Transition Skills and Instructional Strategies: Best Practices

Schoolwork and IEPs must help students to develop specific skills necessary for transitions. Mentors should guide special educators in supporting students as they learn to solve problems, express individual ideas and needs, set goals and plan for reaching those goals, and understand their rights and responsibilities as students. Figure 7.5 provides a list of the skills to teach for transition.

Figure 7.5   Transition Skills

- Self-determination
- Self-knowledge and self-awareness
- Self-management
- Self-sufficiency
- Self-reflection
- Social skills
- Listening skills
- Conflict resolution
- Leadership development
- Presentation skills

Instructional Strategies for Transition

Knowing the desired outcomes and the skills necessary for transition will translate to effectively designing, planning, and implementing instructional strategies to prepare and support students for this process. Mentors can facilitate and assist special educators in developing best practices for transition. Several strategies are outlined in Figure 7.6 as a reference for mentors to use in their support and assistance of teachers regarding successful instructional practices for transition.

Universal Design for Transition

An important component of the Universal Design for Transition (UDT) includes the characteristics of the Universal Design for Learning (UDL). These characteristics are applied to the transition assessment process by linking curriculum standards to authentic tasks that can be taught and assessed. The following is an outline of steps for instructional planning:

1. Identify the transition needs for instruction, assessment, and self-determination.

2. Identify links to academic standards.

3. Identify other transition needs that have not been addressed.

4. Build UDT unit and lesson plans (Thoma, Tamura, Scott, & Doval, 2009).

Cooperative Groups

Students work together to maximize their own and each other's learning. A team member's success depends on both individual effort and the efforts of other group members who contribute necessary knowledge, skills, and resources. One group member cannot possess all of the information, skills, or resources necessary. Individual strengths are utilized.

Peer Coaching and Cross-Age Tutoring

Interaction and dialogue tend to be much more mutual when compared to an adult–child instructional relationship. Participants are more apt to express opinions, ask questions, and take risks.

Student-Centered Focus

The student completes age-appropriate transition assessments in order to accurately identify strengths, preferences, and interests. Student-led IEPs are held on an ongoing basis throughout the year.

Assistive Technology

Greater independence is promoted with the use of assistive technology by enabling individuals to perform tasks that they were formerly unable to accomplish or had great difficulty accomplishing.

Service Learning

Service learning is a link between academic subject matter and community-based/student-directed service projects. The best educational practice incorporates rigorous academic learning while students are engaged in community improvement. Service learning can promote students' success in achieving both academic goals and goals related to transition, while providing transition activities for those students with learning disabilities who are often located in the general education setting (O'Connor, 2009).

Transition Portfolio

Portfolios are based on the concept that learning is a lifelong process. They can serve as a means to teach students with disabilities how to develop a plan of action. The portfolio makes it possible for educators to provide a visible and concrete way of demonstrating the link between school-based learning and preparation for the world of work and adulthood. Several checklists for transition are included in Resource C (see Tools 7.1, 7.2, 7.3, and 7.4) and Internet resources for transition are provided in Figure 7.6. Mentors can share these tools with special education teachers and model the use of them with students. These tools can facilitate student thinking and planning for transitions and also provide helpful information to the teachers and specialists who will be working with the students in the future.

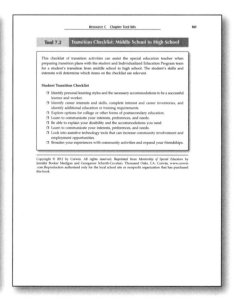

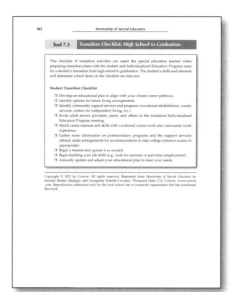

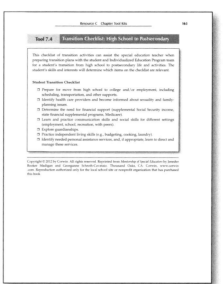

Transition Situations

As mentors are aware, the transitions from elementary school to middle school and from middle school to high school are both transition times that do not require meeting IDEIA regulations but are left to teacher, school, and district best practices. When mentors guide teachers in developing the mind-set of what constitutes a transition, teachers can then help students develop skills and flexibility that enable them to deal with situations successfully. Figure 7.7 provides a look at typical school career transitions and additional situations that involve students making transitions.

Figure 7.6 Internet Resources for Transition

- Transition Coalition: www.transitioncoalition.org (tips database)
- National Center on Secondary Education and Transition: www.ncset.org (resources and technical assistance related to secondary transition available in English and Spanish)
- National Secondary Transition Technical Assistance Center: www.nsttac.org (support and information regarding effective transition education that can enhance postschool outcomes)
- The National Center for Culturally Responsive Educational Systems (NCCRESt): www.nccrest.org/about.html (suggestions for improvements in culturally responsive practices, literacy, and positive behavioral supports)

These ideas of possible additional situations involving transition are for mentors and teachers to consider when developing best practices. Various transition events can be ascertained and plans for instruction can be developed through a brainstorming process between mentors and special educators. This collaborative process helps to determine the many skills and subskills necessary for students to be successful. The mentor then helps with the next steps in the establishment of goals and assessments, which drive and determine ongoing instruction while assisting the special educator in monitoring student progress toward developing lifelong skills for transitions.

Figure 7.7   Transition Situations

School Career Transitions for Students	Transitional Situations for Students
• Birth to age 3 • Age 3 to preschool • Preschool to kindergarten • Elementary to middle school • High school to adult living • Adult to postschool outcomes	• Moving to a new school and/or classroom • Being mainstreamed from a self-contained special education classroom into a general education classroom for part of the day • Going from home to school and back home • Changing from one activity or content area to another • Going from the classroom to recess and then back to the classroom • Transitioning from the school year to summer school and/or vacation • Changing placements (general education student qualifying for special education services or a change from one type of special education service to another) • Changing school schedule from one year to the next

Summary

Life is full of transitions, and special educators facilitate access for all areas of life. Transition goals ought to drive IEPs in order for education to occur in a natural, uncontrived manner. Special educators, with the aid of their mentors, can empower students by designing instruction that will help students to develop self-knowledge and skills that lead to fulfilling experiences. Mentors need to work together with special education teachers to increase knowledge about and sensitivities to the families they serve, using this knowledge as they focus on effective communication and a collaborative and family-centered approach to transition processes. The special education teacher can then in turn share that gained family knowledge with other teachers, specialists, and paraprofessionals who work with the students.

References

Greene, G. (2009, April). *Transition of culturally and linguistically diverse (CLD) youth with disabilities: Challenges and opportunities.* Council for Exceptional Children, 2009 Conference and Expo, Seattle, WA.

Hogansen, J. M., Powers, K., Geenen, S., Gil-Kashiwabara, E., & Powers, L. (2008). Transition goals and experiences of females with disabilities: Youth, parents, and professionals. *Exceptional Children, 74*(2), 215–234.

Individuals with Disabilities Education Improvement Act. 20 U.S.C. § 1400 (2004). Retrieved from http://idea.ed.gov/download/statute.html

O'Connor, M. P. (2009). Service works! Promoting transition success for students with disabilities through participation in service learning. *Teaching Exceptional Children, 41*(6), 12–17.

Rueda, R., Monzo, L., Shapiro, J., Gomez, J., & Blacher, J. (2005). Cultural models of transition: Latina mothers of young adults with developmental disabilities. *Exceptional Children, 71*(4), 401–414.

Thoma, C., Tamura, R., Scott, L., & Doval, E. (2009). *Universal design for transition: An idea whose time has come.* Council for Exceptional Children, 2009 Conference and Expo, Seattle, WA.

Thompson, J. R., Meadan, H., Fansler, K. W., Alber, S. B., & Balogh, P. A. (2007). Family assessment portfolios: A new way to jumpstart family/school collaboration. *Teaching Exceptional Children, 39*(6), 19–25.

8

Collaboration With Paraprofessionals

Joy Kutaka Kennedy

Supervising and managing my aide is challenging. I feel sabotaged by her. She interrupts instruction and doesn't listen when I am giving student directions. My aide doesn't seem to understand what her relationship with students should be. She has difficulty managing groups and modifying the assignment to meet their needs.

—Middle school beginning special education
teacher for sixth-grade self-contained,
cross-category, multilingual, multicultural classroom

Chapter 8 Topics, Activities, and Tools

- Establishing a Collaborative Relationship With Paraprofessionals
- Roles of the Special Education Teacher and the Paraprofessional
- Activities for Mentoring Teachers as They Collaborate With Paraprofessionals
- Activity 8.1. Challenging Situation: The Novice Teacher Meets the Veteran Paraprofessional
- Activity 8.2. Teacher Roles or Paraprofessional Roles
- Activity 8.3. Working With Paraprofessionals

Mentoring special education teachers frequently involves preparing them for the unfamiliar role of supervising paraprofessionals. Often, the roles and responsibilities of the special education teacher and the paraprofessional are vague and ill-defined (French, 2003b; National Education Association, 2000; Pickett, Gerlach, Morgan, Likins, & Wallace, 2007). Teacher preparation programs rarely train special education teachers in their legal supervisory responsibilities and vital instructional leadership roles; this problem is exacerbated by district practices of hiring paraprofessionals and then providing minimal guidance and training for the work expected of them (Hilton & Gerlach, 1997; National Education Association, 2004; Special Education News, 2000). Some special education teachers express frustration that they have been prepared to teach students but are unprepared to train adult paraprofessionals (National Education Association, 2000; Special Education News, 2000).

Similarly, the paraprofessionals who are supervised by freshly minted special education teachers also possess a variety of abilities, skills, experiences, and motivation levels. A special education teacher may be assigned newly hired paraprofessionals, often without his or her input in the interviewing and hiring process (Hilton & Gerlach, 1997; Pickett et al., 2007). Some advocates estimate that 70% to 90% of paraprofessionals are hired without much prior training, and most are trained on the job by their supervising teachers and other paraprofessionals. In contrast, a new special education teacher may be assigned a veteran paraprofessional with 20 years of experience working with numerous new special education teachers. The age and experience differences between the new special education teacher and the experienced paraprofessional can pose certain challenges.

The development of a professional collaborative relationship can prove beneficial for all stakeholders. This chapter provides the mentor with references to possible issues that arise, activities for assisting the educator in developing skills required for supervision and management tasks, and ideas for mentors to facilitate team building and working relationships between special education teachers and paraprofessionals.

Roles of the Special Education Teacher and the Paraprofessional

One of the first areas for mentors to clarify is the role and responsibilities of the special education teacher with his or her classroom

Activity 8.1	Challenging Situation: The Novice Teacher Meets the Veteran Paraprofessional

This activity is designed to promote reflection and discussion regarding how to establish a relationship with one's assigned paraprofessional. The mentor can lead discussion with the teacher about issues related to the development of a mutually respectful, productive relationship.

The mentor can read and discuss the following vignette with the special educator.

Toward the end of her teacher training program, Anna, a recent college graduate, found a job teaching middle school in one of the poorest areas of town with a high percentage of Hispanic, African American, and Puerto Rican students. Anna has read about working with multicultural students, and she is excited to begin teaching in her first self-contained class. She is anxious to meet her assigned paraprofessional, Juana, who has 20 years of experience. Juana lives in the community, speaks Spanish, and understands the local culture. She began her career as a volunteer when her children attended school. Anna is nervous about how she will manage to supervise Juana when she feels like such a novice herself. Anna is intimidated by the breadth and depth of Juana's experience, and she wonders what she should say when she firsts meets Juana.

The mentor can then ask the teacher to reflect on the following questions:

1. How can Anna establish a collaborative dialogue with Juana to develop a climate of positive, open communication?

2. How can Anna set the guidelines and expectations of her paraprofessional's work?

3. How can Anna solicit Juana's assistance in working with her multicultural students, their families, and the community?

4. How can Anna plan for sharing information on collaboration, class rules, behavior management plans, calendars, schedules, Individualized Education Program (IEP) access, monitoring, teaching, and confidentiality provisions?

Based on the reflections from questions one through four, the mentor and teacher can brainstorm a list of ideas or activities for creating a culture of mutual respect between teachers and paraprofessionals.

paraprofessionals. Mentors should emphasize the need for teachers to exercise their legal responsibilities, under the direction of the school district, as classroom instructional leaders, responsible for preparing, planning, scheduling, monitoring, and directing the work of paraprofessionals. A paraprofessional, commonly called a classroom assistant, a teacher aide, an instructional aide, an educational support person, or a paraeducator, is a district employee who *assists* and *supports* teacher-directed instruction and services for the benefit of students and their educational programs (French, 2003a; Gerlach, 2009a).

Paraprofessionals and Diversity

Former secretary of education Richard Riley (1998) argued that schools should reflect the overall makeup of society to promote social justice and equity. Research indicates that culturally and linguistically diverse (CLD) students perform better when they have teachers from similarly diverse backgrounds (Anderson & Madigan, 2005; Gay, 2000; Riley, 1998). The presence of paraprofessionals from diverse backgrounds can remediate some of the deleterious effects of CLD disproportionation between special education teachers and their students. Paraprofessionals often represent the culture of the area and are committed to their community (French, 2003a). Cognizant of the hierarchies involved in the school setting, they know how to navigate the challenges, rewards, social culture, and organizational procedures of schooling; furthermore, paraprofessionals have invaluable experience with students, parents, teachers, and other support staff. Since attracting culturally diverse teachers to work with students from backgrounds of similar diversity is often challenging, developing a local paraprofessional pool is an excellent way to bring diversity awareness to the classroom. Darling-Hammond and Cobb (1996) report that 77% of paraprofessionals came from CLD groups compared to 10% of all entrants into teacher education programs. The paraprofessionals' crucial role as cultural emissaries cannot be overlooked or understated in special education classrooms.

Activity 8.2	Teacher Roles or Paraprofessional Roles

Mentors can provide the following list of activities for the special educators to review and reflect upon. After reflection, mentors can ask special educators to determine which items are teacher roles and which items are paraprofessional roles, followed by a discussion and collaborative planning session.

1. Plan weekly schedule, lessons, room arrangements, learning centers, activities, instructional delivery, materials, resources, and assessments for individuals and the entire class.

2. Support students in performing activities that have been initiated by the teacher.

(Continued)

(Continued)

3. Administer and score formal and informal tests.

4. Reinforce learning with individuals or small groups under teacher direction.

5. Determine appropriate objectives for groups and individual children.

6. Provide special help such as drilling with flash cards, spelling practice, and learning-through-play activities.

7. Observe behavior and then plan and implement behavior management strategies for the entire class and for individual children.

8. Respond to requests for help from students, observe students' learning difficulties, and report this information to teachers.

9. Meet with parents to share information on student progress and initiate conferences with parents and others to meet the child's learning needs.

10. Share ideas and concerns during conferences and carry out duties as directed by a teacher.

11. Arrange time to collaborate, share goals and philosophy, provide relevant training, and organize job duties for the paraprofessional.

12. Assist the teacher with crisis problems and behavior management and provide consistent support to the classroom management plan.

13. Set an example of courtesy and professionalism in execution of teacher responsibilities.

14. Assist in preparing instructional materials, managing resources, and maintaining student records.

Paraprofessionals in the Classroom

In order to help special education teachers to plan for and include paraprofessionals in best educational practices, mentors can reiterate some of the benefits of having paraprofessionals in the classroom that include

- better communication with multicultural students, parents, and community;
- additional positive role models, mentors, and tutors for students;

- supplementary instructional opportunities for students, both individually and in groups;
- increased attention to individual student needs academically, socially, and behaviorally;
- added support for the teacher in planning instruction, assessing learning, and evaluating programs;
- more personnel to support and monitor student progress;
- improved student outcomes, including
  - more positive self-concept,
  - better attitudes toward learning and school engagement,
  - increased motivation to succeed,
  - improved behavior and self-management, and
  - healthier relationships;
- increased teacher morale; and
- beneficial supportive teamwork with other adults.

Mentors should clarify that although the teacher is responsible for training his or her paraprofessionals only for classroom, instructional, behavioral, or clerical support related to the educational needs of the student or program, it is useful to have an understanding and appreciation of the scope of their work. Wearing many hats, a paraprofessional might be asked by the school administrator to perform duties as varied as

- instructional assistance
- English Learner (EL) assistance
- noninstructional or clerical assistance
- one-to-one assistance with students
- library or computer lab assistance
- building, playground, lunchroom, and recess supervision
- preschool caregiving and bus duty
- translation
- serving as a liaison between the school and students' families and between the school and the community (National Education Association, 2004, 2005)

Supervising Paraprofessionals in the Classroom

Generally, the school district administration is responsible for recruiting, hiring, scheduling, assigning, and formally evaluating paraprofessionals; supervising timecards; and facilitating district communications. Teachers, however, usually oversee the day-to-day activities of the paraprofessional. Responsibilities such as introducing the new paraprofessional to the building and staff, the school and district policies and procedures, and legal requirements regarding confidentiality might be fulfilled by the principal or the teacher (Gerlach, 2009a).

Mentors can help the special education teacher clearly understand that paraprofessionals should always be supporting the lesson plans, behavioral interventions, and other programs developed, directed, monitored, and evaluated by certificated or licensed teachers; legally, paraprofessionals cannot independently plan, direct, evaluate, and assess student learning without teacher oversight. However, paraprofessionals can assist in instruction, classroom management, student discipline, student safety, and conflict resolution. They can participate in preparing materials for learning, monitoring student learning, delivering instruction, grading papers, recording scores, motivating students, developing students' social skills, and communicating with parents (French, 2003a; Gerlach, 2009b; National Education Association, 2004, 2005). Paraprofessionals are indispensable in supporting the teacher, students, school, and community.

Building the Special Education Team

Teachers, who function as the chief executive officers of their classrooms, have many responsibilities as team leaders. Besides designing lesson plans to meet the instructional needs of students and working with certificated peers, special education teachers must also collaborate closely with their paraprofessionals. Mentors play a critical role in assisting the special education teacher in the development or enhancement of skills necessary to achieve the extensive responsibilities that come with the position. Mentors can help with organizational strategies, role-play meetings and conversations, and facilitate collaborative efforts between all of the classroom personnel. The following is a list of responsibilities that mentors can observe for and help the special educator plan for, strategize for, and implement.

1. Create an atmosphere of positive team collaboration in which members from diverse multicultural, educational, and socioeconomic backgrounds are valued and respected.

2. Prepare assignments for paraprofessionals based on student needs, program objectives, and the paraprofessionals' skills.

3. Solicit input from paraprofessionals in creating learning activities that provide supportive and inclusive learning environments for children, youth, families, and staff.

4. Involve paraprofessionals in various components of the learning process to support teacher and program functions as well as students' needs.

5. Provide on-the-job training and feedback to prepare paraprofessionals to carry out team decisions.

6. Monitor the day-to-day performance of paraprofessionals.

7. Share relevant information with principals about paraprofessionals' strengths and professional development needs.

8. Engage paraprofessionals in planning and organizing learning experiences based on their qualifications to accomplish the tasks.

9. Train paraprofessionals to extend learning experiences in various environments including classrooms, libraries, study halls, playgrounds, work sites, and community-based settings.

10. Coach paraprofessionals to use the methods, materials, and equipment required to achieve learning outcomes for students with disabilities.

11. Instruct paraprofessionals in informal assessment and record-keeping activities to support student progress.

12. Adhere to the ethical and professional standards of conduct regarding the supervision and evaluation of paraprofessionals established by relevant professional organizations.

13. Model standards of professional and ethical conduct for paraprofessionals (i.e., maintaining confidentiality, demonstrating respect for diverse cultures, and advancing the human, legal, and civil rights of students and their families).

14. Direct paraprofessionals to follow guidelines established by the district and/or state to protect the health, safety, and well-being of learners and staff.

15. Participate in opportunities for professional development that improve supervisory and team-building skills.

16. Train paraprofessionals to foster independence, question for higher-order thinking, diffuse conflicts, implement IEP goals, report student incidents, and record behavioral data.

Activity 8.3	Working With Paraprofessionals

The mentor can ask the teacher to review the previous list of 16 tasks and select which will be easiest and which will be most difficult to implement. After reviewing the teacher's responses, the mentor and the teacher can discuss ways to build on the teacher's strengths and develop an action plan for implementation of team building with the paraprofessionals.

It behooves the special education teacher to make efforts to recognize and validate the important contributions of his or her paraprofessionals. Mentors can assist special education teachers to have clearly defined job descriptions that will facilitate the working relationships in their classroom. When all team members in the classroom know what is expected, it is easier for everyone to do their job well. When asked what is important to them in their daily work aside from the rewards of working with students, paraprofessionals identified two major outcomes: recognition for the vital role they play and respect for their professionalism (National Education Association, 2004).

Summary

Mentoring special educators requires a multitude of skills, abilities, dispositions, and sensibilities. Teachers come with a wide range of life experiences and skill levels including teaching, supervising, evaluating, team building, and collaborating. Developing an effective collaborative team can be one of the most rewarding aspects of working as a special education teacher aside from nurturing and observing the growth of one's students. This chapter provided an overview of some of the issues, challenges, and solutions for mentors in guiding special education teachers through the process of developing meaningful communication and effective collaboration with their paraprofessionals. Mentors play an important role in guiding, advising, and supporting special education teachers in their efforts to create positive relationships with their paraprofessionals. Effective communication, adequate planning, and understanding are major keys to productive collaboration not only with paraprofessionals but with other professionals as well.

References

Anderson, M. G., & Madigan, J. (2005). *Research to practice brief: Creating culturally responsive classroom environments.* Tampa: University of South Florida. http://www.ldonline.org/article/Creating_Culturally_Responsive_ Classroom_Environments?theme=print

Darling-Hammond, L., & Cobb, V. (1996). The changing context of teacher education. In F. Murray (Ed.), *The teacher educator's handbook.* San Francisco: Jossey-Bass.

French, N. (2003a). Managing paraeducators. In A. L. Pickett & K. Gerlach (Eds.), *Supervising paraeducators in educational settings: A team approach* (2nd ed.). Austin, TX: Pro-Ed.

French, N. (2003b). Paraeducators in special education programs. *Focus on Exceptional Children, 36*(2), 1–16.

Gay, G. (2000). *Culturally responsive teaching.* New York: Teachers College Press.

Gerlach, K. (2009a). *Let's team up! A checklist for paraeducators, teachers, and principals* (6th ed.). Washington, DC: National Education Association of the United States.

Gerlach, K. (2009b). *The paraeducator and teacher team: Strategies for success— paraeducator supervision participant workbook* (11th ed.). Tacoma, WA: Pacific Lutheran University.

Hilton, A., & Gerlach, K. (1997). Employment, preparation, and management of paraeducators: Challenges to appropriate service for children with disabilities. *Education and Training in Mental Retardation and Developmental Disabilities, 36*(2), 71–76.

National Education Association. (2000). *The NEA paraeducator handbook.* Washington, DC: Author.

National Education Association. (2004). *Results-oriented job descriptions: How paraeducators help students achieve.* Washington, DC: Author.

National Education Association. (2005). *Paraeducators and IDEIA 2004: Knowledge, skills advocacy training guide.* Washington, DC: Author.

Pickett, A. L., Gerlach, K., Morgan, M. L., Likins, M., & Wallace, T. (2007). *Paraeducators in schools: Strengthening the educational team* (2nd ed.). Austin, TX: Pro-Ed.

Riley, R. (1998). Our teachers should be excellent, and they should look like America. *Education and Urban Society, 31*(1), 18–29.

Special Education News. (2000). *Many teachers say they are not prepared to coach paraeducators.* Retrieved from http://www.specialednews.com/educators/ednews/parateams051900.html

9

Collaboration With Professionals

As the year continues, one type of support I need to receive from my mentor is collaborating/communicating with other teachers.

—Beginning special education
teacher of K–5 students

S tatements from special education teachers show their need of support throughout the process of collaboration with general educators, administrators, and other specialists involved with the special education team. Collaboration can be implemented in many different ways in both general and special education classrooms, including collaboration with other teachers or specialists, school and district personnel, general educators, or community members. This chapter will highlight excerpts from the Individuals with Disabilities Education Improvement Act (IDEIA) related to professional collaboration, review a framework of models of coteaching, and define a possible schoolwide collaborative model. Additionally, suggestions and activities for mentors to use with teachers are provided for improving the collaboration process.

Individuals with Disabilities Education Improvement Act Requirements

The importance of building collaborative partnerships among general educators, special educators, parents, and administrators to assist a child with special needs is addressed extensively in IDEIA. Mentors play a critical role in supporting special educators in the development of collaborative relationships. Figure 9.1 highlights the key points

Activity 9.1	Individuals with Disabilities Education Improvement Act Regulations and Collaboration

Mentors and the special educators can review IDEIA regulations in this chapter related to collaboration between specialists, administrators, general educators, agencies, and other support organizations. The teacher can make a list of terms in the regulations such as collaborative and consultative models, early intervention, and related services. The mentor can provide definitions and clarification of terms for the special educator. Together, the mentor and teacher can formulate ideas about effective methods of collaboration between various professionals and supporting agencies.

Figure 9.1   Individuals with Disabilities Education Improvement Act: Collaboration and Professional Development

1. Reduction of

   a. the paperwork burden on teachers, principals, administrators, and related service providers; and

   b. noninstructional time spent by teachers in complying with part B;

2. Enhancing longer-term educational planning

3. Improving positive outcomes for children with disabilities

4. Promoting collaboration between Individualized Education Program (IEP) team members

5. Ensuring satisfaction of family members

And

Professional.Development Activities. A state educational agency that receives a grant under this subpart shall use the grant funds to support one or more of the following:

1. Carrying out programs that provide support to both special education and regular education teachers of children with disabilities and school administrators, such as programs that

   a. provide teacher mentoring, team teaching, reduced class schedules and caseloads, and intensive professional development;

   b. use standards or assessments for guiding beginning teachers that are consistent with challenging state student academic achievement and functional standards and with the requirements for professional development; and

   c. encourage collaborative and consultative models of providing early intervention, special education, and related services.

2. Providing professional development activities that

   a. provide training in how to teach and address the needs of children with different learning styles and children who are limited English proficient, and

   b. involve collaborative groups of teachers, administrators, and, in appropriate cases, related services personnel.

And

Personnel Development: Enhanced Support for Beginning Special Educators. The secretary shall support activities

   a. for personnel development, including activities for the preparation of personnel who will serve children with high-incidence and low-incidence disabilities, to prepare special education and general education teachers,

> principals, administrators, and related services personnel (and school board members, when appropriate) to meet the diverse and individualized instructional needs of children with disabilities and improve early intervention, educational, and transitional services and results for children with disabilities; and
>
> b. for enhanced support for beginning special educators. (Individuals with Disabilities Education Improvement Act, 2004)

from the IDEIA regulations related to collaboration and professional development for teachers, administrators, and parents that mentors can share with special education teachers.

Collaboration: Challenges and Solutions

Challenges for the Special Education Teacher

Collaboration between special educators and general educators is often hindered by a lack of planning time (Bouck, 2007; Carpenter & Dyal, 2007; Paulsen, 2008). Other barriers to collaboration include a lack of personnel to share the work, a lack of preservice teacher training in working with other adults, a resistance to change, and a lack of training related to teacher roles in collaborative partnerships (Paulsen, 2008). The mentor can provide information and resources for the teacher related to collaboration and encourage the teacher to participate in professional development that facilitates the selection of appropriate collaborative strategies (Carpenter & Dyal, 2007).

Solutions: Collaboration in the Classroom Through Coteaching

The relationships cultivated between general educators and special educators are the foundation of the trust and rapport that will lead to collaborative coteaching in the classroom. Mentor support will be a key component in the successful implementation of a coteaching model of instruction. Friend and Bursuck (2009) describe five options teachers typically use when implementing a coteaching model:

1. Lead and support

2. Station teaching

3. Parallel teaching

4. Alternative teaching

5. Team teaching

When working with teachers, mentors can introduce and model the five options. Figure 9.2 provides a reference for mentors to use with teachers that highlights the key aspects of each type of coteaching.

Figure 9.2   Five Coteaching Models

Lead and Support

One teacher leads, and another offers assistance through support to individuals or small groups. Planning includes both teachers, but typically one teacher plans for the lesson content while the other does specific planning for students' individual learning or behavioral needs.

Station Teaching

Students are divided into heterogeneous groups; each group works at a classroom station with one of the teachers. At a designated time, students switch to the other station. In this model, both teachers individually develop the content of their stations.

Parallel Teaching

Teachers jointly plan instruction. Instruction is delivered simultaneously by each teacher to half the class or a small group. This model requires joint planning time to ensure that as teachers work in their separate groups, they are delivering content in the same way.

Alternative Teaching

One teacher works with a small group of students to preteach, reteach, supplement, or enrich instruction while the other teacher instructs the large group. More planning time is needed to ensure that the logistics of preteaching or reteaching can be completed.

Team Teaching

Both teachers share the planning and instruction of students. Similar knowledge of the content, a shared philosophy, and a commitment to all students in the class are critical. This model takes time to develop and can occur effectively when teachers work together over an extended period of time.

Activity 9.2	Development of a Vision for Coteaching

The mentor and special education teacher can discuss the listed five components for successful coteaching and develop a shared vision of what a successful coteaching relationship would include in the teacher's working environment. The mentor can encourage the teacher to write specific goals for coteaching and a summary of his or her philosophy of inclusion.

Following are five critical components for successful coteaching:

1. Shared planning time for general and special educators
2. Similar level of content knowledge to make the model work effectively
3. A shared philosophy of inclusion
4. Common goals
5. Trust and respect

Collaboration With Educators and Specialists

Special educators typically lead and direct IEP meetings (Martin et al., 2006). Some specialists (e.g., transition counselors and speech and language therapists) are frequently not invited to attend or collaborate in the IEP team process (Agran, Cain, & Cavin, 2002). The role of the school psychologist is sometimes not clearly understood or articulated. Often, due to time constraints, psychologists perform assessments independently and do not communicate the assessment results or recommendations with the special educator and other team members until the IEP meeting. These factors can contribute to inconsistencies and misunderstanding between the IEP team members. Other challenges to effective collaboration include personality differences between the special educator and specialists, differing expectations and outcomes for students, a lack of value for another's professional status, and an inadequate amount of resources and time (Hartas, 2004; Hemmingsson, Gustavsson, & Townsend, 2007). The mentor will be a critical partner in supporting the special education teacher through the first IEP meetings. The follow-up activity below will assist the mentor in guiding the teacher through potential scenarios that can arise.

Activity 9.3	Collaboration and Problem Solving With Individualized Education Program Team Members

Mentors and special educators can role-play various scenarios that may occur in an actual Individualized Education Program meeting. The mentor can guide the teacher through situations such as the following:

1. Disagreement between an administrator and a general educator about the placement of a student

2. A request from a parent for services that may not be plausible for the special education teacher to deliver

3. A conflict between the special education teacher and another specialist, such as a transition counselor, about a student's upcoming placement

These scenarios can be based on actual situations the teacher is involved in or possible situations that could occur in the future, depending on the special education teacher's position. The purpose of the activity is to guide the teacher toward optimal collaboration between specialists, administrators, general educators, agencies, and other support organizations.

Collaboration in the School Setting: Professional Learning Communities

Many school districts have adopted the Professional Learning Communities (PLC) model. This model addresses the necessity for collaborative efforts leading to effective schools and student achievement. Mentors can provide teachers with information about PLCs as a framework for understanding systemic collaboration. Figure 9.3 can be used to provide the mentor with an overview of PLCs.

Special educators may find themselves assigned to collaborative teams, meeting with teams during the school day, providing intervention instruction, and/or participating in professional development using a PLC model or an RTI model if they are fortunate enough to be working at such schools. Within any collaborative role, the teacher may find that colleagues look to him or her for leadership in assessment, analysis, and/or intervention strategies. Discussions and activities to develop the special educator's confidence for

Figure 9.3   Professional Learning Communities

According to DuFour, DuFour, and Eaker (2008), the main ideas that frame a Professional Learning Community (PLC) include the following:

- Ensuring that *all* students learn at a high level
- Building a collaborative culture in which school personnel work interdependently, taking collective responsibility for the learning of all students
- Systematically monitoring student learning on an ongoing basis in order to quickly respond to students experiencing difficulty

Schools that implement a PLC model have in place structural conditions and social resources such as

1. time for teachers to meet during the day,

2. organized collaborative teams of teachers,

3. common goals,

4. open communication,

5. trust and respect,

6. sharing of practices, and

7. supportive leadership (DuFour et al., 2008).

The PLC model addresses the Individuals with Disabilities Education Improvement Act requirements and recommendations in that they share common areas of focus. Similarly, the federally stipulated services of the Response to Intervention (RTI) initiative (see Chapter 7 for details of RTI) follow suit with the PLC model's systematic monitoring of student learning and instructional intervention (DuFour et al., 2008).

collaboratively working with colleagues are important for the mentor to facilitate. Mentors can support special educators in their collaborative roles by providing resources such as a variety of formative assessment tools, practicing analysis of student work together, participating in the collaborative team meetings, and discussing strategies of intervention. In addition, mentors might organize and arrange visitations to experienced teachers' classrooms in order for special education teachers to observe a variety of intervention strategies firsthand. The teacher would then have a repertoire of observed experiences to share with colleagues within his or her role as a collaborative team member as well as ideas to apply to his or her own teaching. Prior to visiting experienced teachers' classrooms, it's important to establish learning outcomes of the visits and set some goals; following

Figure 9.4   Observation Guide

Mentor Conversation Points	Elements for Teacher to Observe
• Determine area of focus and desired outcomes of observation with teacher • Inquire what was noticed and main ideas learned • Ascertain the experienced teacher's classroom application • Find out if the special education teacher has any further questions	• Classroom environment • Routines and procedures • Classroom management • Transitions, pacing, and use of time • Teaching and instructional strategies • Teacher questioning techniques • Student engagement

the visits, discussion to coach for application of what was learned will be beneficial. Figure 9.4 provides a framework for mentor use with special education teachers.

Summary

Communication and open pathways for professional dialogue create an environment for delivery of high-quality educational experiences for every member of a school community. Professional collaboration between IEP team members is an essential component for delivering the best possible special education plan to a student. The regulations in IDEIA related to building collaborative partnerships have provided a range of opportunities for enhanced special education teamwork through the reduction of paperwork, professional development, and enhanced support for special educators. The role of the mentor in this very critical area of development with special educators includes reviewing the IDEIA regulations; discussing the roles of various education professionals (administrators, school psychologists, general educators, and other specialists); and planning ways, based on best practices, to implement these strategies and communicate practices to parents.

References

Agran, M., Cain, H. M., & Cavin, M. D. (2002). Enhancing the involvement of rehabilitation counselors in the transition process. *Career Development for Exceptional Individuals, 25*(2), 141–155.

Bouck, E. C. (2007). Co-teaching . . . not just a textbook term: Implications for practice. *Preventing School Failure, 51*(2), 46–51.

Carpenter, L. B., & Dyal, A. (2007). Secondary inclusion: Strategies for implementing the consultative teaching model. *Education, 127*(3), 344–350.

DuFour, R., DuFour, R., & Eaker, R. (2008). *Revisiting professional learning communities at work™: New insights for improving schools.* Bloomington, IN: Solution Tree.

Friend, M. P., & Bursuck, W. D. (2009). *Including students with special needs: A practical guide for classroom teachers* (5th ed.). Upper Saddle River, NJ: Pearson Education.

Hartas, D. (2004). Teacher and speech-language therapist collaboration: Being equal and achieving a common goal? *Child Language Teaching and Therapy, 20*(1), 33–54.

Hemmingsson, H., Gustavsson, A., & Townsend, E. (2007). Students with disabilities participating in mainstream schools: Policies that promote and limit teacher and therapist cooperation. *Disability & Society, 22*(4), 383–398.

Individuals with Disabilities Education Improvement Act. 20 U.S.C. § 1400 (2004). Retrieved from http://idea.ed.gov/download/statute.html

Martin, J. E., Van Dycke, J. L., Greene, B. A., Gardner, J. E., Christensen, W. R., Woods, L. L., et al. (2006). Direct observation of teacher-directed IEP meetings: Establishing the need for student IEP meeting instruction. *Exceptional Children, 72*(2), 187–200.

Paulsen, K. J. (2008). School-based collaboration: An introduction to the collaboration column. *Intervention in School and Clinic, 43*(5), 313–315.

10

Communication With Parents

Terry Halterman Jr.
and Jennifer Madigan

I will welcome the parent to our conference by . . . thanking the parent for taking time and being so willing to meet and work together to support her son. [Information to elicit from the parent includes asking . . .] Are there any routines at home for homework completion? What does it look like? Science homework is more difficult for the student, and it may be better if it is completed in his tutorial class at school.

—Middle school special education teacher for
Grades 7 and 8 in multilingual, cross-category,
self-contained core subject and tutorial classes

Chapter 10 Topics, Activities, and Tools

- Mentoring Special Education Teachers Toward Creating Positive Communication Between Home and School
- Strategies for Overcoming Challenges to Communication Between Teachers and Parents
- Activity 10.1. Individuals with Disabilities Education Improvement Act and Parent–School Communication
- Activity 10.2. Perspectives: An Analysis of Beliefs and Experiences

C omments from special education teachers reveal the need for assistance in developing a communication network between the teachers and parents of students with special needs from culturally and linguistically diverse (CLD) backgrounds. This chapter will highlight relevant legislative regulations from the Individuals with Disabilities Education Improvement Act (IDEIA) related to parental involvement and rights in the special education process. Recommendations for mentor use with teachers will be discussed and a management system for facilitating the communication process will be presented.

Special education teachers need a range of different kinds of support from mentors when assuming new classroom positions. Among the most important relationships teachers establish are partnerships with parents of special education students. The mentor plays a critical role in guiding the special education teacher through this process. IDEIA has added specific guidelines for schools and educators to assist parents of children with disabilities. Figure 10.1 and Activity 10.1 can be utilized by the mentor to assist the teacher in understanding the IDEIA regulations and strategizing together how to build collaborative relationships between the special education teacher and the parents.

Figure 10.1   Working With Parents: The Individuals with Disabilities Education Improvement Act

According to the regulations published in the Federal Register effective July 2006, parent training and information activities assist parents of a child with a disability in dealing with the multiple pressures of parenting and are of particular importance in

  a. Creating and preserving constructive relationships between parents of children with disabilities and schools by facilitating open communication between the parents and schools, encouraging dispute resolution at the earliest possible point in time, and discouraging the escalation of an adversarial process between the parents and schools;

  b. Ensuring the involvement of parents in planning and decision making with respect to early intervention, educational services, and transitional services;

  c. Achieving high-quality early intervention, educational results, and transitional results for children with disabilities;

(Continued)

Figure 10.1 (Continued)

d. Providing parents with information about their rights, protections, and responsibilities under this title to ensure improved early intervention, educational results, and transitional results for children with disabilities;

e. Assisting parents in the development of skills to help them participate effectively in the education and development of their children and in the transitions described in section 673(b)(6);

f. Supporting the roles of parents as participants within partnerships seeking to improve early intervention, educational services, and transitional services and results for children with disabilities and their families; and

g. Supporting such parents who may have limited access to services and support due to economic, cultural, or linguistic barriers (Individuals with Disabilities Education Improvement Act, 2004).

In order for personnel development to improve services and results for children with disabilities, personnel may be trained in the innovative uses and application of technology, including universally designed technologies, assistive technology devices, and assistive technology services:

- To enhance learning by children with low-incidence disabilities through early intervention, educational services, and transitional services
- To improve communication with parents (Individuals with Disabilities Education Improvement Act, 2004)

Activity 10.1	**Individuals with Disabilities Education Improvement Act and Parent–School Communication**

1. Mentors and special education teachers can read together the information located within the Individuals with Disabilities Education Improvement Act (IDEIA) in Figure 10.1 related to communication between parents and the school.

2. Mentors and teachers can brainstorm together a list of ideas for developing positive communication between home and school. Then they can select three specific activities for implementation. The mentor can work with the teacher in the development and implementation of the selected activities. One example of an activity is included in Resource C as Tool 10.1.

Challenges to Communication: Communicating With Parents From Culturally and Linguistically Diverse Backgrounds

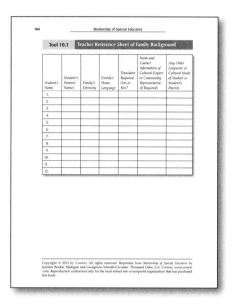

Many teachers struggle with creating a climate of effective communication and collaboration with families and the communities they serve. Mentors can assist the special educator by pointing out some of the possible barriers that may exist between the school and home environments. The following key points can provide a starting place for discussion between the mentor and teacher.

1. Communication

a. The native language of a family may deter communication between the special education teacher and CLD parents (Lo, 2008; Tellier-Robinson, 2000).

b. Educational jargon may seem confusing to CLD parents and present barriers to effective dialogue (Miles-Bonart, 2002; Valle & Aponte, 2002).

c. Families may lack knowledge of how the special education system functions and may need additional time to process information provided to them at meetings concerning their children (Zhang & Bennett, 2003).

2. School Culture

a. Communication between CLD parents and teachers may be hindered by a cultural acquiescence to the perceived authority of school professionals; some CLD parents may feel intimidated by Individualized Education Program (IEP) meetings or may not be invited to the IEP meetings at all (Harry, 2008; Torres-Burgo, Reyes-Wasson, & Brusca-Vega, 1999).

b. Mutual misconceptions about and lack of trust in CLD families and school professionals may limit effective communication between both parties (Harry, 2008).

c. Differing viewpoints on appropriate goals for students with disabilities may also impede any effort toward productive communication between CLD parents and school staff (Harry, Klingner, & Hart, 2005).

These challenges represent a few of the complex and multifaceted scenarios that can impact a teacher's efforts to establish a climate of effective communication between home and school. The following section will address specific strategies mentors can offer to special education teachers to promote meaningful dialogue and collaboration with students, families, and their communities.

Preparation and Organization: Tips for Effective Communication Between Teachers and Culturally and Linguistically Diverse Families

Mentors can encourage special education teachers to employ a range of strategies to promote meaningful and effective communication between home and school. The following suggestions are grounded in research related to best practices for working with parents from CLD backgrounds:

1. The teacher should be aware of the English proficiency, literacy level, and interaction methods of CLD parents (Dennis & Giangreco, 1996).

2. A translator may be necessary to facilitate communication between school and home for some CLD parents. Besides bridging the language barrier, the use of a translator may augment the parents' trust level (Conroy, 2007).

3. Teachers should avoid using educational terms and jargon that may be unfamiliar to parents and ensure that parents understand the terms and acronyms used by the IEP team (Miles-Bonart, 2002).

4. Communication with CLD families may be best facilitated by (a) becoming cognizant of others' cultures and histories, and (b) analyzing one's own perspective as well as the perspective of

the special education field as a whole concerning disabilities and the expertise of those working in the field (Harry, 2002, 2008).

5. Making use of a cultural expert or a community representative can also facilitate the communication process between CLD parents and teachers by informing teachers about beliefs of the family and the culture with which the family identifies (Barrera & Kramer, 2009; Dennis & Giangreco, 1996).

Activity 10.2	Perspectives: An Analysis of Beliefs and Experiences

This activity is designed to promote reflection and discussion between the mentor and special education teacher on issues related to perceptions of culture and disability. The mentor and teacher can write and share reflective responses to the following questions:

Reflect and write about your experiences in school as a child with peers from different cultures or backgrounds and peers with disabilities.

How have these experiences shaped your ideas today about culture and disability?

What would you like your students and their families to know about your culture and history? What are some ways you can share your story with your students and their families?

Brainstorm a list of ideas and activities for creating a culture of mutual respect in your classroom by recognizing and honoring differences and similarities between school staff, students, families, and the community.

Summary

Effective communication and collaboration with families is one of the most important areas of development and growth for special education teachers. The role of mentors in this process is crucial for the success of teachers in their efforts to build a bridge between the school and home environments. This chapter provided an overview of some of the challenges and solutions for mentors to consider in guiding special education teachers through the process of developing meaningful communication and collaboration with their students, families, and the community.

References

Barrera, I., & Kramer, L. (2009). *Using skilled dialogue to transform challenging interactions: Honoring identity, voice, and connection.* Baltimore, MD: Brookes.

Conroy, P. W. (2007). Hmong culture and visual impairment: Strategies for culturally sensitive practices. *RE:View, 38*(2), 55–64.

Dennis, R. E., & Giangreco, M. F. (1996). Creating conversation: Reflections on cultural sensitivity in family interviewing. *Exceptional Children, 63*(1), 103–116.

Harry, B. (2002). Trends and issues in serving culturally diverse families of children with disabilities. *Journal of Special Education, 36*(3), 131–138.

Harry, B. (2008). Collaboration with culturally and linguistically diverse families: Ideal versus reality. *Exceptional Children, 74*(3), 372–388.

Harry, B., Klingner, J. K., & Hart, J. (2005). African American families under fire: Ethnographic views of family strengths. *Remedial and Special Education, 26*(2), 101–112.

Individuals with Disabilities Education Improvement Act. 20 U.S.C. § 1400 (2004). Retrieved from http://idea.ed.gov/download/statute.html

Lo, L. (2008). Chinese families' level of participation and experiences in IEP meetings. *Preventing School Failure, 53*(1), 21–27.

Miles-Bonart, S. (2002, March). *A look at variables affecting parent satisfaction with IEP meetings.* Paper presented at the Annual National Conference Proceedings of the American Council on Rural Special Education (ACRES), Reno, NV.

Tellier-Robinson, D. (2000). Involvement of Portuguese-speaking parents in the education of their special needs children. *Bilingual Research Journal, 24*(3), 309–323.

Torres-Burgo, N., Reyes-Wasson, P., & Brusca-Vega, R. (1999). Perceptions and needs of Hispanic and non-Hispanic parents of children receiving learning disabilities services. *Bilingual Research Journal, 23*(4), 373–387.

Valle, J. W., & Aponte, E. (2002). IDEIA and collaboration: A Bakhtinian perspective on parent and professional discourse. *Journal of Learning Disabilities, 35*(5), 469–479.

Zhang, C., & Bennett, T. (2003). Facilitating the meaningful participation of culturally and linguistically diverse families in the IFSP and IEP process. *Focus on Autism and Other Developmental Disabilities, 18*(1), 51–59.

Conclusion

The need for support of special educators in today's schools is critical. We believe our book has addressed key elements of focus for those professionals working with mentors and/or teachers, with the goal of student achievement at the core. The intended outcome for this book was to provide a pertinent and relevant resource for professional developers and mentors, as well as a practical and ready-to-use handbook with organizational tools and guidance for educators working with diverse learners. The chapter topics highlighted essential components for effective mentoring and effective teaching and addressed contemporary issues that currently exist in schools and classrooms.

In our writing and research for this publication, three core descriptors have emerged:

1. Strategic

2. Systematic

3. Deliberate

We believe that successful mentoring and instruction encompass approaches that include ingredients of strategic, systematic, and deliberate implementation. Evidence of these key ideas has been illustrated in the following manner:

Strategic

Chapter 4, Supporting Student Learning, concentrated on strategic and culturally relevant teaching approaches through differentiation of instruction and implementation of the Universal Design for Learning

(UDL) for student achievement. It is essential for mentors to develop strategic, critical questions for teacher growth in pedagogy in order to address individual student needs. Resources, tools, and activities were included for support in this area. **Chapter 7, Transition,** described strategies for transitions in all areas of a student's life, including sensitivity to families, effective communication, and a family-centered approach to transitions. **Chapter 9, Collaboration With Professionals,** highlighted essential components for providing high-quality special education planning for a student in the context of professional collaboration through the implementation of specific strategies for effective teamwork.

Systematic

Chapter 3, Beginning of School, Scheduling, and Planning Individualized Education Programs, addressed organizational components for the myriad of roles special educators perform and focused on the critical function of mentors as they support teachers in the establishment of systems related to management of paperwork, communication, teaching, and assessment. **Chapter 5, Response to Intervention and Positive Behavior Support,** provided resources for understanding the range of Response to Intervention (RTI) systems in addition to the role special educators play in academic and behavioral interventions that are systematically implemented. **Chapter 10, Communication With Parents,** emphasized systems that build bridges between the school and home environment.

Deliberate

Chapter 1, Mentorship of Today's Special Educators, and **Chapter 2, Mentor and Teacher Relationship,** focused on the deliberate development of relationships between mentors and special education teachers through the identification of expectations and roles on the part of participants. In addition, effective methods for mentors to address and support needs of teachers and inspiration for creating thoughtful teaching practices were presented. Deliberate development of habits of mind for ongoing reflective practice was discussed. **Chapter 6, Culturally Competent Assessment,** provided an overview of best practices related to culturally competent assessment, with an emphasis on the deliberate use of alternative assessments for culturally and linguistically diverse (CLD) students. **Chapter 8, Collaboration With Paraprofessionals,** offered activities for the mentor and special educator to engage in to deliberately help develop important skills needed for collaboration with paraprofessionals.

Deliberate, systematic, and strategic actions by mentors have an influential impact on the special education teacher's professional development. Consequently, teachers are empowered, knowledgeable, and proficient in guaranteeing opportunities for student achievement. We are confident that this book will be an important and useful tool for skillful mentoring for special educators.

Resource A

Professional Development Case Studies for Mentors

Christine Hagie

Activity A.1   Working With Paraprofessionals

When school started in August, a paraprofessional (sometimes this position is called an instructional associate or instructional aide), Ms. Madonna, was assigned to work with you full-time. You were also told that another paraprofessional, Mr. Prince, would be with you for one hour each day. These two individuals started working on the first day of class; you met each new paraprofessional at the same time as the students did.

Working with these two individuals has been very challenging. They are friends outside of work, and when they are together in the classroom, they talk about nonclassroom things such as weekend plans or their latest music interests. Mr. Prince takes direction, however, and can be redirected to complete his duties during the hour he is in the class. But Ms. Madonna has a difficult time staying focused on the activities that she has been assigned. You observe her texting on her phone several times each day, she is late at least one day each week by 20–25 minutes, and she delivers harsh reprimands to the students.

You don't have any time to talk with the paraprofessionals without students present. Planning with them seems impossible, and there is no time in the day to talk about the activities expected or the things that you want them to do in your program. You have learned from the principal that Ms. Madonna has worked in the school for several years and prides herself on making good connections with students. She started volunteering in a special education class when she was in high school, and her father is a school principal. She is very creative and has talent in art. Mr. Prince is working part-time while he goes to law school in San Francisco. His schedule is very full (even though he seems to have time to party on the weekends with Ms. Madonna). He is interested in special education law and the mandates that guide the education process.

Everyone tells you to "document" things that are problematic, but you do not know what to do with this documentation. The principal told you to "deal with it" when you asked for guidance because these two individuals are protected in their jobs by their tenure and contracts.

What will you do?

Activity A.2 | Planning Lessons and the Curriculum

When your mentor arrives at the school to visit you, the principal, Ms. Hardcore, dashes out of her office and intercepts her to talk about your lesson planning (or lack of lesson planning). Ms. Hardcore requires weekly lesson plans from each of the teachers in the school; she holds high standards for the teachers in terms of lesson planning and connecting lessons and curriculum to content standards. The mentor explains that you are a special education teacher and currently just learning how to develop lessons, but this does not fly with Ms. Hardcore. She requests that the mentor observe you teaching and write recommendations for improvements that specifically relate to lesson planning.

You need to develop a process and format for lesson planning to submit to the principal. Describe how you will do this and develop the format that you will use.

Activity A.3 | Managing Stress and Stressful Situations

Finally, it is spring. You started this job in late August and have worked very hard in the three classes you are taking, as well as planning each evening for the next day. You like your students a lot; if it weren't for them, this job would be very difficult. Throughout the year, it seemed that the administration added students to your class every month, which was very hard (nobody can tell you the maximum number of students that can be in your program). There is typically little to no warning when you're going to get a new student, except for an Individualized Education Program (IEP) meeting weeks or sometimes days before, which you are usually not able to attend.

As you reflect, you are bothered by several of the IEP meetings that you have attended for your students. In one situation, the administrator in the meeting told the parents of your student that the child does not need speech and language services and that budget constraints make it difficult to hire a qualified speech therapist. In another meeting, there was not an interpreter for the parents and so they attended the meeting but did not participate; you suspect it was because they do not know English. Last week, an administrator told a mother that her son just needs more discipline at home and then his behavior would improve at school. She had requested a meeting to talk about the poor reports coming from school about her son's behavior.

You realize that you are having trouble sleeping lately, and you suspect that it is because of these situations. What are some things that you can do to stay in this job and get some sleep (or feel as if you can maintain ethical professionalism)?

Activity A.4	Getting It All Done While Maintaining Sanity

They told you that there would be a lot of work, including your own classes each week, your homework, and your new job as a first-year teacher. But you are feeling much more overwhelmed than expected. Each day as you drive to campus, you try to make a mental list of all that you need to do before hitting the pillow that night (after your class ends at 10 p.m.) and before your students arrive the next morning at 7:45 a.m. You have three triennial Individualized Education Program (IEP) meetings in the next week, and you have to admit to yourself that you are not even sure what a triennial IEP is, let alone how to develop the paperwork and plan the meeting. You had instruction about this in your preservice training, but you forgot where you put the notes. Your family and friends are worried about you, and their concern is only adding to your stress.

Last week, you turned in an assignment one week late and you forgot to add to the online discussion board for another class. You are worried that you are falling behind with the course work, and you do not know how to manage the situation. You are really embarrassed that you actually cried when you talked with the intern coordinator at the university.

Clearly, you need to make some sort of plan to complete your course work, plan and develop lessons for your students, and do all of the other expected tasks related to the IEP process. What will you do?

| Activity A.5 | **What Are Individualized Education Programs?** |

In the second week of your new job, you have been told that the annual review of three of the Individualized Education Programs (IEPs) for your students are months late, and you have two "tris" (triennial reviews) that are due. You are not really sure what these are, let alone what is expected of you. You look online and find thousands of links about the process for an IEP, but you don't really know how to begin, and the twenty or so links that you reviewed are not helpful. You have been told that your county is adopting a web-IEP system that will help you write the document. But when you went to the training, the computer system was down, and you had to go home.

You did, however, attend one IEP meeting with a student who might start in your class. You asked your mentor to attend with you, but she was busy. A psychologist seemed to be in charge of the meeting, and the IEP document was many pages long. The team was unhappy that a general education teacher was not available to attend the meeting, and several people you have not met came into the room and sat in the meeting for 10 minutes or so, signed one of the pages of the form, and left. You really do not understand the process. You need to know the legal process for the IEP meeting and your role in the process. How will you get some help?

| Activity A.6 | Dealing With Challenging Behaviors |

Develop your own group case study. Describe either a student's challenges with behavior or a group or class that has behavior problems. Describe the challenges on this page: include a description of the problem, baseline data and documentation of the problem, guesses about the function of the problem, and ideas for interventions.

1. Description of the Problem

2. Baseline (How often does this happen?)

3. Possible Function of the Behavior

4. Ideas for Intervention

| **Activity A.7** | **Brainstorming Activity** |

Title of the Case Study: _____

Teachers in the Group: _____

_____

_____

Date: _____

Read the case study and then brainstorm some solutions for this situation (write ideas on this paper). Have you experienced anything like this in your current teaching position? Discuss your job with the group members. Evaluate each of the possible interventions, and develop a list of suggestions to deal with this challenge.

Activity A.8	**Evaluation of Case Study**

Date: _____

The one new thing I learned today is . . .

I felt that the case study activity was . . .

Comment on the participation of everyone in your group:

A concern that I have about my job is . . .

I would like to talk about or get more information about . . .

Resource B

Teacher Retention and Peer Mentoring

A Model for Success

Christine Hagie

One of the most important things for me in keeping my sanity and perspective about my job, and the tough situations I deal with, is the support I get from other special ed. teachers. I couldn't do what I do without that.

—High school special education teacher in a
multilingual, diverse school teaching
core subjects and tutorial classes

This section highlights the features of a special education teacher preparation program that places an emphasis on mentoring in the context of peer-to-peer support or *peer mentoring*. The extent to which special education intern teachers feel confident in their jobs possibly relates to the support they receive from peers or other interns. In an alternative (intern) teaching preparation program in northern California, interns find great comfort in working together. During the two-year intern program, the interns requested increased structure for seminars to discuss common situations and challenges of the job while sharing ideas.

This section begins with a brief review of the research and then moves on to an explanation of the support provided by veteran teachers to interns in the Collaborative Intern Program prior to the development of Intern Support Seminars. It also explains the history and the steps for development of the seminars using case studies created from focus groups in which interns discussed the most pressing challenges in the first year of teaching. Finally, a summary of feedback and evaluation from interns about the Intern Support Seminars is presented. A tool kit that includes Intern Support Seminar case studies and worksheets is provided in Resource A.

The Importance of Peer-to-Peer Support

A preponderance of the research about teacher retention and attrition suggests that lack of or little support for new teachers might contribute to a decision to leave the profession (Billingsley & Cross, 1991; Brownell & Smith, 1993; Fimian & Santoro, 1983; Gersten, Keating, Yovanoff, & Harniss, 2001; Griffin et al., 2009; Miller, Brownell, & Smith, 1999; Whitaker, 2003). Most of the support identified by the teachers in these studies focuses on administrators or even teacher preparation programs rather than support from peers. There are fewer studies investigating the support needs of teachers who provide special education services, and there is little research that has a specific focus on teacher-to-teacher support.

Several studies, however, have examined the influence of collegial relationships with peers on successful special education teachers. Kilgore and Griffin (1998) interviewed four teachers in their first, second, and third years of special education teaching and found that a challenge they all faced was a lack of enough support personnel. Whitaker (2003) conducted five focus groups with new special education teachers, mentors, and administrators to identify teachers' needs. She found that they wanted both scheduled and unscheduled meetings with mentors, they wanted to be observed and given feedback, and they needed someone who was readily available to provide support. Special education teachers were surveyed about the influences on their choice to stay in the job (Gersten, Keating, Yovanoff, & Harniss, 2001), and one aspect that led to unhappiness in the job was found to be stress, which could be decreased with support from other teachers. New teachers in a South Carolina study in which 156 teachers were surveyed reported that other special education teachers provided the most help for them in their new jobs (Whitaker, 2003).

Teachers participating in the Study of Personnel Needs in Special Education (SPeNSE) reported that the most valued support was from their peers (Billingsley, Carlson, & Klein, 2004). In California, teacher retention and attrition was the focus of a large study with 2,000 teachers responding to an online survey (Futernick, 2007). They reported that support from peers or other teachers was an important factor that influenced their decision to stay in the job; former teachers participating in the study reported that "inadequate system supports" (Futernick, 2007, p. viii) posed problems for them when they were in the job.

During a group interview with veteran teachers of students with emotional disturbances who had been in the job for many years, interviewees were asked if they remembered a time when they wanted to leave the job. All participants smiled as they nodded *yes*; when asked what made them stay in their jobs for so many years, each individual simultaneously pointed to another teacher in the circle, indicating it was peer support that made the difference (Hagie, 2001).

Support Provided to Interns Prior to the Development of Intern Support Seminars

Interns in the Collaborative Intern program are supported and mentored by university supervisors and by district-assigned mentors who hold matching credentials and have at least three years of teaching experience. Each intern communicates with his or her mentor on a regular basis through scheduled meetings, e-mails, phone conversations, and/or informal get-togethers. Mentors can keep notes on a contact form to summarize the content of each interaction and remind each party of the next steps.

The type of support from the district mentor and the university supervisor can include the following, depending on the needs of the new teacher:

1. Discussing items such as classroom setup, Individualized Education Program (IEP) document writing, positive behavior support plans, curriculum ideas, instructional strategies, available resources, school district procedures and policies, and work with families

2. Providing emotional support for any aspect of the job

3. Observing the intern teaching and providing feedback and/or coaching

4. Responding to questions that the intern might have about the job

5. Communicating regularly through e-mail to check in with the intern

6. Discussing the process to access materials or curriculum and/or providing resources for the intern

7. Accompanying the intern to observe a master teacher

8. Demonstrating teaching techniques, assessments, IEP collaboration, and/or use of specific curricular materials

The district mentor typically has more of a focus on the district or school policies and procedures, while the university supervisor focuses more on methodologies and techniques for the classroom and with the students. The intern, the mentor, and the university supervisor identify the type and frequency of contacts and support for their relationship.

In the first semester of the program, the intern identifies three objectives that address the areas in which he or she wants to improve over the 15-week semester, proposes the activities to assist in meeting the objectives, and provides baseline ratings for those areas in his or her own teaching. At the end of the semester, each intern summarizes his or her progress on the objectives, reflects about the process, identifies additional goals (if appropriate), and provides data or evidence indicating that each objective was met. This process continues for each of the four semesters until an intern completes the first tier of the credential, or Level I (in California).

History of Peer Support in the Collaborative Intern Program

The teacher preparation program includes four credential programs: the mild to moderate disabilities credential, the moderate to severe disabilities credential, the early childhood special education credential, and the deaf and hard of hearing credential. There is an intern option for each program, in which students complete all required course work to earn a California teaching credential while working as a teacher over two years.

Participants in the Collaborative Intern Program typically do not take all courses as a cohort because they represent the four different special education credential programs, and students are required to take some classes that are not common requirements for all of the programs. Also, many interns enter the program having already completed a number of courses. There are, however, several courses in which all interns participate. It was observed that the interns taking the courses together supported each other in class and seemed to connect with each other outside of class.

Each intern enrolls in a course during the first semester during which the university supervisor visits the new interns' class and they participate in three seminars. During the seminars, interns discussed the following:

- University course work and any secrets about staying on top of the work,
- Their new jobs and any helpful ideas for learning to be a special education teacher on the job, and
- Life outside of school and stress-relieving activities.

The discussions were very lively, and collegial interactions were observed between the interns. Several of the new teachers requested an alumni group after the class ended so that they could continue with the discussions.

During the following semester, interns could participate in the five optional Intern Support Seminars, discussing the following three items:

1. What are the most challenging parts of your job this semester that were unanticipated?

2. What are the biggest rewards of the job at this point?

3. Please share any new ideas or suggest curriculum or materials that you have found useful.

The interns participating in the seminars were from the four different credential programs, and the age range of their students was from birth to age 22. They taught in public elementary, middle, and high schools; nonpublic schools; and charter schools. These were entirely heterogeneous groups, yet the discussion was about issues that they experienced across the teacher preparation programs and across the variety of schools. Again, feedback from the Intern Support Seminars said that they were valuable and promoted collegial relationships between teachers and across credential areas and schools.

It seemed that many of the interns who did not participate in the Intern Support Seminars were struggling in their jobs and in keeping up with the course work. After the second semester of the optional Intern Support Seminars, it was mandatory for all interns not enrolled in a supervision class to enroll in a Support Seminar.

Steps for Development of Intern Support Seminars

Three focus group interviews were conducted with 13–16 second-year interns to determine ways to improve the credential program. The following questions were asked during each session:

- What are the challenges you experienced in the second year of teaching that you did not expect? You may not have had these challenges in the first year, or you may not have even noticed them in the first year.
- Could you share any useful strategies or solutions that you developed for these challenges? Were they successful?

The interns talked about the challenges, and they enthusiastically described their work and the difficulties that were present in the second year of teaching. The participants agreed that they had different challenges in the second year and that they were "clueless" about what the challenges were in the first year. They seemed to also support each other with their responses and discussion. For example, one intern talked about the frustration of learning a new web-based IEP system, and another intern responded with some ideas for learning the new process and offered some help. An intern got very emotional when talking about the stress of taking classes and learning the new job at the same time. Her peers responded with offers of forming a study group for one of the classes, and several talked about their process for studying, planning for the classroom, and having some fun on the weekends. Several interns shared that they had gotten married in the previous months, and a discussion followed about experiencing many changes at once, with suggestions for how to explain the work to a spouse or to friends.

Review of the transcripts indicated the following six areas that were of concern for interns in each of the three focus groups.

1. Working with paraprofessionals

2. Lesson planning

3. Meetings in which parents are told (by school administrators) things that don't sound fair or even legal

4. Completing all of the work for courses and for the new job

5. The IEP process

6. Challenging student behavior

A new one-unit course was developed from the focus group themes, notes recorded during the optional Intern Support Seminar discussions, and intern feedback about the type of support that interns need. The course description, as found on the syllabus, is as follows:

> This course is designed for interns from each of the four credential programs who are in their 2nd and 3rd semesters or who are not currently in a supervision course, EDSE 105, or the last student teaching course. Supervision will be provided during this meeting. Interns will discuss challenging aspects of their jobs and will problem-solve solutions to case studies that describe common situations from former interns in the program. They will update and reflect about their Induction Plan goals. An important objective for this class is for the interns to provide support to each other. (Hagie, 2009, p. 1)

The objectives of the Intern Support Seminars are to provide opportunities for interns to

1. Discuss the challenges and successes of the job with peers,

2. Learn and practice the skills of problem-solving actual situations described by previous groups of new interns, and

3. Develop networks of support with fellow new teachers.

It was important for the interns to talk about real problems or actual situations in this seminar and to avoid participating in complaint sessions. Case studies were developed from the stories recorded in the focus groups. Actual situations that the previous group of interns experienced were put together into a format that provided a guide for each Intern Support Seminar, and an activity worksheet (Activity A.7, "Brainstorming Activity") was developed that guided the discussion; the interns recorded the results of the session on this sheet. Interns from the four different teacher credential programs were divided into heterogeneous small groups for some of the case study activities and into grade-level groups for other case study activities. In the heterogeneous groups, an intern teaching preschool or toddlers, for example, would work in a group with high school teachers of deaf students. In the grade-level groups, all high school teachers worked together, and all middle school teachers worked together.

A sixth session about challenging student behavior was an optional activity in which the interns developed the case study about difficult behavior that at least one intern in the group was experiencing in class.

Feedback and Evaluation of Intern Support Seminars

At the end of each seminar, interns completed an evaluation sheet that provided feedback about the session. Results from the Spring 2009 semester indicated that the sessions were very successful for meeting the objectives of the Intern Support Seminar. By the end of the semester, the participants entered the classroom with hugs, some brought materials to share, and they exchanged phone numbers and e-mail addresses.

References

Billingsley, B., & Cross, L. (1991). Teachers' decisions to transfer from special education to general education: A critical review of the literature. *Journal of Special Education, 27,* 137–174.

Billingsley, B. S., Carlson, E., & Klein, S. (2004). The working conditions and induction support of early career special educators. *Exceptional Children, 70*(3), 333–347.

Brownell, M., & Smith, S. (1993). Attrition/retention of special education teachers: Critique of current research and recommendations for retention efforts. *Teacher Education and Special Education, 15,* 229–248.

Fimian, M. J., & Santoro, T. M. (1983). Sources and manifestations of occupational stress as reported by full time special education teachers. *Exceptional Children, 49,* 540–543.

Futernick, K. (2007). *A possible dream: Retaining California's teachers so all students learn.* Sacramento: California State University.

Gersten, R., Keating, T., Yovanoff, P., & Harniss, M. K. (2001). Working in special education: Factors that enhance special educators' intent to stay. *Exceptional Children, 67,* 549–567.

Griffin, C. C., Kilgore, K. L., Winn, J. A., Otis-Wilborn, A., Hou, W., & Garvan, C. W. (2009). First-year special educators: The influence of school and classroom context factors on their accomplishments and problems. *Teacher Education and Special Education, 32*(1), 45–63.

Hagie, C. (2001). *Teachers of students with emotional disturbances: A study examining factors contributing to a high attrition rate* (Unpublished doctoral dissertation). University of California, Berkeley.

Hagie, C. (2009). *EDSE 105 intern support seminar syllabus.* San Jose, CA: San Jose State University.

Kilgore, K. L., & Griffin, C. C. (1998). Beginning special educators: Problems of practice and the influence of school context. *Teacher Education and Special Education, 21*, 155-173.

Miller, M. D., Brownell, M., & Smith, S. W. (1999). Factors that predict teachers staying in, leaving, or transferring from the special education classroom. *Exceptional Children, 65*(2), 201–218.

Whitaker, S. D. (2003). Needs of beginning special education teachers: Implications for teacher education. *Teacher Education and Special Education, 26*(2), 106–117.

Resource C

Chapter Tool Kits

Tools	Page Number	Brief Description
Tool 2.1. Teacher Information Form	130	This form is for mentors to record information for each teacher; it provides personal information that can be helpful for the mentor in developing relationships with individual teachers.
Tool 2.2. Meeting Notes Recording Form	131	This recording form helps to direct conversation during mentor/teacher meetings about what is working and why and what is not working and why, along with next steps and who will do what and when.
Tool 3.1. Caseload List	132	This is an organizer for mentors to help teachers systematize their caseloads in order to determine schedule of service.
Tool 3.2. Individualized Education Program Timeline Checklist	133	This is a graphic organizer that mentors can provide to help teachers keep track of tasks, forms, and important dates for planning Individualized Education Program meetings.
Tool 3.3. Progress Report	134	This is a resource mentors can provide teachers that solicits general education teachers' input in order to assist special education teachers in writing reports of present levels and progress reports.
Tool 3.4. School Year Individualized Education Program Schedule	135	Mentors can provide this form to teachers to assist in planning Individualized Education Program meetings for the whole year with school psychologists and other specialists as well as creating an "at-a-glance" schedule distinguishing annuals and triennials.

Tools	Page Number	Brief Description
Tool 3.5. Planning Calendar Example	137	This is an example for mentors to share with teachers to help in organizing all of the components of Individualized Education Program planning: permissions to send home, dates for sending notices of meetings, assessments to administer, and so on.
Tool 3.6. Individualized Education Program Meeting Agenda	139	This is an outline for mentors to provide teachers for facilitation of Individualized Education Program meetings with succinct time frames.
Tool 3.7. Individualized Education Program Summary Example	140	This is a communication tool mentors can provide teachers that addresses key descriptors of a student, including eligibility statement, strengths, challenges, accommodations, goals, and dates of Individualized Education Program meetings. The summary form is a snapshot that focuses on key elements of an Individualized Education Program for teachers, parents, and others working with the student in the current or next setting the student will transition to.
Tool 3.8. Student Profile	142	This is designed for mentors in helping teachers to organize information about students on their caseloads for student groupings and monitoring student progress toward goals.
Tool 4.1. Universal Design for Learning Guidelines	143	This tool is a checklist for mentors and teachers to use while collaborating on lesson design, after conferencing, and for teacher self-reflection to ensure that instruction includes multiple means or representation, action and expression, and engagement. In addition, for each listed item, the online version provides an instant link to the Universal Design for Learning website for additional resources.
Tool 5.1. Response to Intervention Pyramid of Intervention	145	This graphic describes the tiers of intervention for a Response to Intervention model for the mentor to use in explaining and ensuring that teachers understand the process and their roles.
Tool 5.2. Twelve Steps for Interventions	146	This template can be used as the mentor collaborates with teachers and teachers collaborate with colleagues in planning the WHO, WHAT, HOW, and WHEN of interventions for students.

(Continued)

Tools	Page Number	Brief Description
Tool 5.3. Student Success Team Referral	150	By sharing this form with special education teachers, mentors help them to become familiar with the information general educators supply when referring a student to the Student Success Team. Special education teachers can use this information to familiarize themselves with a student. Mentors and teachers can also use this information to discuss recommendations for the student.
Tool 5.4. Response to Intervention Flowchart	152	This flowchart clearly identifies the process of Response to Intervention and defines the roles of the team members. Mentors can share with teachers to explain the process and to assist in understanding and planning for next steps.
Tool 5.5. Response to Intervention: Intervention Examples	153	Mentors can provide these examples of interventions at each of the tier levels in the Response to Intervention model. Teachers can then offer these suggestions to team members and classroom teachers and make use of them personally in their intervention work with students.
Tool 5.6. Student Intervention Summary	154	This form can be used to summarize student interventions that mentors can share with teachers for data collection and record keeping.
Tool 5.7. Academic/ Behavior Pyramid	156	Mentors can provide this graphic in helping to explain how behavior interventions follow the same process in a Response to Intervention model.
Tool 5.8. Positive Behavior Support Observation Form	157	Modeling the use of this form by the mentor will assist the special education teacher in observation and data collection for the purpose of behavior intervention. Data collected with this form include antecedent, latency, frequency, duration, intensity, and topography.
Tool 5.9. Student Observation of Behavior	158	This resource can be provided by mentors for teachers' use in assisting students to reflect on their behavior and helping students make progress toward use of replacement behaviors.
Tool 5.10. Behavior Progress Monitoring	159	This form can be used by adults in the student's environment to monitor targeted behavior. This helps with consistency and communication between school and home. Mentors can provide this resource for special education teachers' use.

Tools	*Page Number*	*Brief Description*
Tool 7.1. Fifteen Skills for School and Work	160	This is a transition skill resource for mentors to share with teachers. This form allows students to compare and contrast the skills needed in the classroom with those needed in the workplace. This is a good activity to use when students ask questions such as, "Why do I have to do this math?"
Tool 7.2. Transition Checklist: Middle School to High School	161	This is a checklist of transition activities for mentors to assist the special education teacher when preparing plans for a student's transition from middle school to high school.
Tool 7.3. Transition Checklist: High School to Graduation	162	This is a checklist of transition activities for mentors to assist the special education teacher when preparing students' transitions from high school to graduation.
Tool 7.4. Transition Checklist: High School to Postsecondary	163	This is a checklist of transition activities for mentors to assist the special education teacher when preparing plans for a student's transition from high school to postsecondary life.
Tool 10.1. Teacher Reference Sheet of Family Background	164	Mentors can help teachers to gather information about the families of the students on their caseloads. This tool is extremely valuable in assisting teachers in communication with families and knowing the culture of their students.

Tool 2.1 | Teacher Information Form

Teacher

Name:

Home Address:

Home Phone:

Home E-mail:

Cell Phone Number:

Education Background:

Work Experience:

Volunteer Experience:

Birthday:

Interests/Hobbies:

Favorite Snack:

School Site

School:

Grade Level(s):

Room Number:

School E-mail:

Start Time:

Break Times:

Prep Period:

Lunch Time:

Dismissal Time:

School Address:

School Phone Number:

School Fax Number:

Office Contact Name
and Phone Number:

Administrator/
Principal Name, E-mail,
and Phone Number:

Tool 2.2   Meeting Notes Recording Form

Teacher: _____   Date: _____

What Is Going Well (+)	What Can Go Better (−)
Action Plan	What, Who, When

Next Meeting Date: _____

Tool 3.1	Caseload List

Name	Grade	Teacher/ Room Number	Goal Content Area	Minutes of Service	Individualized Education Program (IEP) Date

Tool 3.2   Individualized Education Program Timeline Checklist

Student's Name	Individualized Education Program (IEP) Date — Tri or Annual	Notice of Referral/ Proposed Action — Date Sent to Parents	Assessment Plan — Date Sent to Parents	Date Parent Permission Received	Notice of Individualized Education Program (IEP) Meeting — Date Sent to Parents	Notice of Individualized Education Program (IEP) Meeting — List of Service Providers, Teachers, and Administrator(s) and Date Sent	Student Assessment — Beginning/ Ending Dates	Date Individual Education Program (IEP) Sent to District Office
1.								
2.								
3.								
4.								
5.								
6.								
7.								
8.								

Tool 3.3 Progress Report

I will be having an Individualized Education Program meeting for this student very soon. I need your input so that I can include this information in my report. Please return this form to _____.

Name of Student _____

Behavior in Class:

Peer Relationships:

Academic Strengths and Weaknesses:

Homework Completion:

Current Grade:

Attendance:

Other Comments or Impressions:

Teacher _____ Date _____

Source: Merchant, K., Felton, CA: North Santa Cruz County Special Education Local Plan Area.

Tool 3.4   School Year Individualized Education Program Schedule

September	Date	Type	Designated Instruction and Service (DIS)	October	Date	Type	DIS	November	Date	Type	DIS
EXAMPLE: John Doe	9/20/11	Triennial	Occupational Therapy (OT)								
December	Date	Type	DIS	January	Date	Type	DIS	February	Date	Type	DIS

(Continued)

(Continued)

March	Date	Type	DIS	April	Date	Type	DIS	May	Date	Type	DIS
June	Date	Type	DIS								

Source: Merchant, K., Felton, CA: North Santa Cruz County Special Education Local Plan Area

Tool 3.5	Planning Calendar Example

2012	Monday	Tuesday	Wednesday	Thursday	Friday	Saturday/Sunday
October	1 Contact administrator and other specialists to confirm John B.'s annual and Sue K.'s triennial dates	2 Give progress report form to John's general education teacher	3 Send invitation/notice of meeting to John B.'s parents and team members	4	5 Observe John in variety of settings Collect work samples	6/7
	8 Send assessment report to Sue K.'s parents	9	10	11	12 Administer Curriculum Based Assessments (CBAs) to John Administer components of Woodcock Johnson III Tests of Achievement (WJIII) to Sue K.	13/14
	15 Send invitation/notice of meeting to Sue K.'s parents and team members	16 Give progress report form to Sue's general education teacher	17	18	19 Write Present Level Report for John and draft of goals Administer CBAs to Sue	20/21
	22	23	24	25	26 Administer components of WJIII to Sue K.	27/28

(Continued)

(Continued)

2012	Monday	Tuesday	Wednesday	Thursday	Friday	Saturday/Sunday
November	29 **John B.** **Annual**	30	31	1	2 Observe Sue in variety of settings Collect work samples	3/4
	5	6	7	8	9 Write reports for Sue and draft of goals	10/11
	12 Send home copy of Sue's assessment report	13	14	15	16 **Sue K.** **Triennial**	17/18

Tool 3.6	Individualized Education Program Meeting Agenda

I.	Introduction of members	3 minutes
II.	Purpose of Individualized Education Program (IEP)	2 minutes
III.	Review previous outcomes (if appropriate)	10 minutes
IV.	Present level of functioning	
	A. Health (developmental history/medical issues)	5 minutes
	B. Cognitive development (observation of responsiveness to environment and problem-solving strategies)	5 minutes
	C. Pre-academic/academic skills	10 minutes
	D. Communication development (speech articulation and oral motor, expressive, and receptive language)	5 minutes
	E. Gross/fine motor skills	5 minutes
	F. Self-help skills (eating, dressing, toileting, etc.)	5 minutes
	G. Social/emotional development	5 minutes
V.	Student strengths	5 minutes
VI.	Parent concerns	5 minutes
VII.	New/continuing goals and objectives	10 minutes
VIII.	Placement and services	5 minutes

Tool 3.7 — Individualized Education Program Summary Example

IEP Summary for: Harry Guess

Annual IEP Date: 1/23/10

Next Triennial: 1/23/12

Grade Level: 5th

Eligibility

Other Health Impairment ~ medical diagnosis of Sturge-Weber Syndrome (impacts visual perceptual and fine motor integration)

Service

Language Arts and Math

Special Education ~ 70 minutes × 5 = 350 minutes

Strengths

Harry's classroom behavior is excellent. He has many friends in class. Harry always tries his best and works hard on any activity. He has made excellent improvement in math. Harry's attendance and homework completion are both good. He has a *great* sense of humor.

Challenges/Concerns

Harry has little to no vision in his right eye. Although he has many friends in class, he doesn't have a close buddy. Harry has experienced teasing from others outside of class. Writing is a struggle. Harry at times gets VERY frustrated and angry and clenches his fists, shutting down for a time until he cools off.

Classroom Accommodations/Strategies

- Seat close to the front of the room
- Allow more time to complete tasks
- Modify homework **by providing materials with enlarged print and reduction in number of problems**
- Vary the length of student work periods
- Encourage and reward progress on a task to motivate and maintain momentum

California Standards Test/Districtwide Assessment Accommodations

1. Large-print booklet for standardized testing

2. Extra time on test within a testing day

3. Test over more than one day for a test part that is to be administered in a single setting

4. Supervised breaks within a section of the test

5. Administration of the test at the most beneficial time of the day for the student

6. Math test questions read aloud to student

Goals

Math

1. By 1/23/10, Harry will demonstrate fluency and proficiency when given 20 problems requiring a variety of math computation including division with positive integers, long division with multidigit divisors, multidigit multiplication, decimals, and fractions with 90% accuracy in 2 of 3 trials as measured by student work samples/criterion assessment.

Language Arts

1. By 1/23/10, after completing a first draft, Harry will edit and revise for coherence by adding, deleting, consolidating, and/or rearranging text to produce an edited version that scores at least 3 on the writing rubric in 2 of 4 trials as measured by student work samples.

2. By 1/23/10, when given a narrative or expository reading passage at the fifth-grade level, Harry will read the passage with appropriate pacing, intonation, and expression at a rate of 120 correct words per minute with 96% accuracy in 3 consecutive trials as measured by student work samples/teacher-charted records.

3. By 1/23/10, when given dictated/written text assignments, Harry will spell roots, suffixes, prefixes, contractions, and syllable constructions correctly with 80% accuracy in 2 of 4 trials as measured by student work samples/teacher-constructed assessments.

Tool 3.8   Student Profile

Student/ Grade Birth Date	Qualification	Goals	English Language Level: Beginning, Intermediate, Advanced	Special Services	Reading Level	Math Level	Evidence Goals Met

Tool 4.1 | Universal Design for Learning Guidelines

Universal Design for Learning (UDL) Guidelines	Unit/Lesson: _____
I. Provide Multiple Means of Representation: Recognition Networks	
1. Provide Options for Perception (Examples)	Your Ideas
1.1. Customize the display of information	
1.2. Provide alternatives for auditory information	
1.3. Provide alternatives for visual information	
2. Provide Options for Language and Symbols	Your Ideas
2.1. Define vocabulary and symbols	
2.2. Clarify syntax and structure	
2.3. Decode text and mathematical notation	
2.4. Promote crosslinguistic understanding	
2.5. Illustrate key concepts nonlinguistically	
3. Provide Options for Comprehension	Your Ideas
3.1. Provide or activate background knowledge	
3.2. Highlight critical features, big ideas, and relationships	
3.3. Guide information processing	
3.4. Support memory and transfer	
II. Provide Multiple Means for Action and Expression: Strategic Networks	
4. Provide Options for Physical Actions	Your Ideas
4.1. Provide varied ways to respond	
4.2. Provide varied ways to interact with materials	
4.3. Integrate assistive technologies	
5. Provide Options for Expressive Skills and Fluency	Your Ideas
5.1. Allow choices of media for communication	

(Continued)

(Continued)

Universal Design for Learning (UDL) Guidelines	Unit/Lesson: _____
5.2. Provide appropriate tools for composition and problem solving	
5.3. Provide ways to scaffold practice and performance	
6. Provide Options for Executive Functions	**Your Ideas**
6.1. Guide effective goal setting	
6.2. Support planning and strategy development	
6.3. Facilitate managing information and resources	
6.4. Enhance capacity for monitoring progress	
III. Provide Multiple Means for Engagement: Affective Networks	
7. Provide Options for Recruiting Interest	**Your Ideas**
7.1. Increase individual choice and autonomy	
7.2. Enhance relevance, value, and authenticity	
7.3. Reduce threats and distractions	
8. Provide Options for Sustaining Effort and Persistence	**Your Ideas**
8.1. Heighten salience of goals and objectives	
8.2. Vary levels of challenge and support	
8.3. Foster collaboration and communication	
8.4. Increase mastery-oriented feedback	
9. Provide Options for Self-Regulation	**Your Ideas**
9.1. Guide personal goal setting and expectations	
9.2. Scaffold coping skills and strategies	
9.3. Develop self-assessment and reflection	

Source: Center for Universal Design. (2008). *Principles of universal design.* Retrieved from http://www.design.ncsu.edu/cud/about_ud/udprincipleshtmlformat.html#top

Response to Intervention Pyramid of Intervention

2011-12 SCESD Pyramid of Intervention

III . Intervention Program and Targeted Assistance

– Read 180, Gateways, *Language!*
– Some Special Ed Students

At-Risk Students
–Two years below grade level

–Intensive

RSP
SDC
SL
Students not Qualifying

Acad. Enrich
Summer School
Inter-Sessions
Saturaty Academies

Before/After School Programs
(i.e., SES and Site-Basd)

Mentor , Tutor , Peer Tutoring
Core ELA and/ or Math Intervention (15-30 mins.)

• Individual Learing Folder

Instr . Aides

• Push In

General Education Resource Teacher.

Behavior

• (i.ef, behavior contract, counseling, 504 Plan,ect.)

Class Size Reduction (as funds available)

Intervention

II. Core Curriculum plus Supplemental Curriculum

– General Ed Specialist
– Special Support

– General Ed Resource Teacher
– Instructional Aide

Struggling Students

–Strategic
–Intensive

ELD

Language Arts............
   – Universal Access.........

Math............
P.E..............
Music
Science/Health Ed.
Social Studies

60 min. by lang. proficiency levels

• 2.5 hr (Pr. Gr.)/2hr.(Upp. Gr):
   (30 minutes):

   • Challenge – Enrichment
   • Benchmark – Independent (85%)
   • Strategic/Intensive – Classroom Teacher
   • 60 minutes
   • 200 minutes within 10 days

Extended Curriculum

Core + Supplemental

Home Classroom Teacher
(Differentiated Homework)

I. Core Curriculum

III

II

I

All Students:
General and Special
   Education
   – Challenge
   – Benchmark
   – Strategic
   – Intensive

Source: Dr. Juvenal Luza, Slainas City Elementary School District, Salinas, CA.

Tool 5.2   Twelve Steps for Interventions

1. Identify the need(s) that the intervention will be addressing.

Needs	Evidence of Needs

2. Define the goals of the intervention.

Goals	Intervention	Prevention

3. Create the intervention.

Describe Intervention	List Components

4. Define the absolute nonnegotiables of the intervention.

Absolute Nonnegotiables	What Will Happen Without Failure	Discretionary

5. Define your system.

a. How will you make your intervention systematic?
b. Describe how you will guarantee student access to the intervention.

6. Identify the discussions you need to have.

Prioritized Topic Order	With Whom?	When?
1.		
2.		
3.		
4.		
5.		
6.		
7.		
8.		
9.		
10.		

7. Identify roles and assign accountability.

Name	Role	Person Accountable

(Continued)

(Continued)

8. Decide on your incremental timelines and your process.

What Needs to Be Accomplished?	By When?	What Process Will You Use?

9. Finish/complete the "Whatever It Takes" Intervention Plan Worksheet.

a. What questions still need to be considered and answered?

b. What is left to determine or decide?

10. Define your TWO Cycles of Success (assessment, intervention, monitoring): one for the intervention, one for the students.

Intervention

Who Will Assess, Intervene, and Monitor?	Frequency	Informal Assessment	Formal Assessment

Student

Who Will Assess, Intervene, and Monitor?	*Frequency*	*Informal Assessment*	*Formal Assessment*

11. Create your plan for stakeholder buy-in.

Plan for Buy-in	*Stakeholder*	*Written Plan*	*Verbal Plan*

12. Add this intervention to your Pyramid of Intervention and review the effectiveness of your other interventions and their relationship to this one.

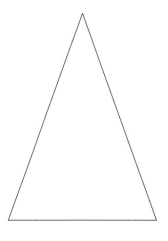

Source: Dr. Juvenal Luza, Slainas City Elementary School District, Salinas, CA.

Tool 5.3   Student Success Team Referral

Date: _____ Teacher: _____ Grade: _____ Room: _____

Student

Last Name: _____ First Name: _____

Gender: _____ Date of Birth: _____

Parent or Guardian: _____ Address: _____

Home Phone Number: _____ Cell and Work Phone Numbers: _____

Home Language: _____ Migrant? _____ Yes _____ No

Areas of Concern (Please Prioritize)

_____ Behavior   _____ Language   _____ Fine/gross motor
                                                                    skills

_____ Math   _____ Attendance
                                                   _____ Other

_____ Written language _____ Social/emotional
                                        skills

_____ Reading

Please Describe Concerns

Areas of Strength

Parent and Professional Communications

Spoke with _____ on _____.
Concerns discussed:

Spoke with _____ on _____.

Concerns discussed:

Spoke with _____ on _____.

Concerns discussed:

Review Cumulative File Attach: Student Intervention Records,
Assessment Data, and Work Samples

Language Dominance: English _____ Spanish _____ Other
(specify language) _____

Standards-Based Assessments (Level and Scaled Score): English Learner Scores (if
applicable):   _____   Math: _____

Reading Fluency Rate: _____   Other: _____

Math: _____ Below Grade Level _____ At Grade Level
_____ Above Grade Level

Notice of risk of failure sent: _____ No _____ Yes (specify date sent): _____

School History

Has the student been retained? _____ No _____ Yes (specify grade): _____

Current Number of Absences: _____ Current Number of
Tardies: _____ Past Truancy: _____

Number of Suspicions: _____ Number of Schools Attended: _____

Last School Attended: _____

Language of Instruction (SEI—Sheltered English Immersion, AP—Bilingual, DI—Dual
Immersion): _____

_____ Kindergarten _____ First Grade _____ Second Grade _____
Third Grade _____ Fourth Grade _____ Fifth Grade _____ Sixth Grade

Health Information

Vision Test Date and Result: _____ Glasses: _____ Yes _____ No

Hearing Test Date and Result: _____ Allergies: _____

Special Medication: _____

Recurring Illness or Disease: _____

Other Health Information: _____

Other Significant Information

Source: Dr. Juvenal Luza, Slainas City Elementary School District, Salinas, CA.

Tool 5.4   **Response to Intervention Flowchart**

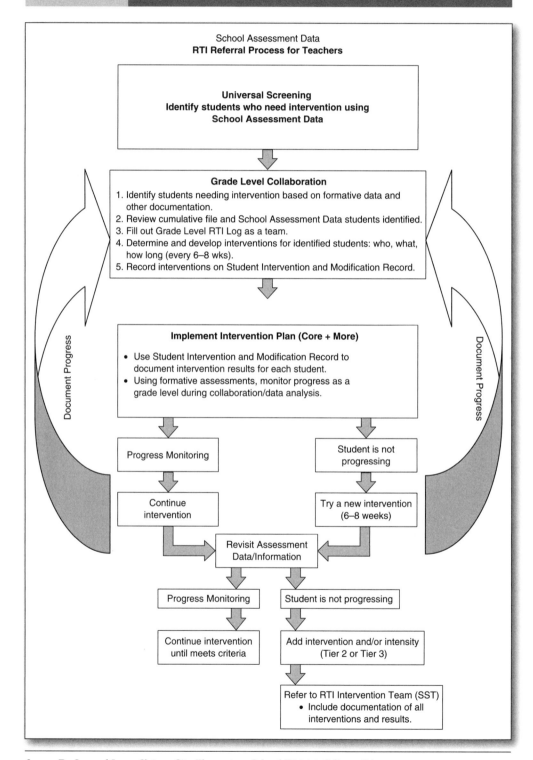

School Assessment Data
RTI Referral Process for Teachers

Universal Screening
Identify students who need intervention using
School Assessment Data

Grade Level Collaboration
1. Identify students needing intervention based on formative data and other documentation.
2. Review cumulative file and School Assessment Data students identified.
3. Fill out Grade Level RTI Log as a team.
4. Determine and develop interventions for identified students: who, what, how long (every 6–8 wks).
5. Record interventions on Student Intervention and Modification Record.

Implement Intervention Plan (Core + More)

• Use Student Intervention and Modification Record to document intervention results for each student.
• Using formative assessments, monitor progress as a grade level during collaboration/data analysis.

Document Progress

Progress Monitoring

Student is not progressing

Continue intervention

Try a new intervention (6–8 weeks)

Revisit Assessment Data/Information

Progress Monitoring

Student is not progressing

Continue intervention until meets criteria

Add intervention and/or intensity (Tier 2 or Tier 3)

Refer to RTI Intervention Team (SST)
• Include documentation of all interventions and results.

Source: Dr. Juvenal Luza, Slainas City Elementary School District, Salinas, CA.

Tool 5.5	Response to Intervention: Intervention Examples

Tier 1: In-Class Essential Standards-Based Interventions

- Guided reading
- Audiobooks
- Vocabulary instruction
- School-adopted reading-based curriculum
- Reading fluency practice
- Online programs

Note: Students of concern are discussed with grade-level collaborative teams to establish interventions.

Tier 2: Small-Group Targeted Skill Interventions

- Reading comprehension peer tutoring
- Small-group instruction (by academic concern; i.e., grade-level teachers exchange students)
- Individual learning folders
- Push-in resource and/or paraprofessional support
- Peer tutoring
- Afterschool, intersession, summer, and/or Saturday Academy programs
- Parent involvement

Note: Possible Student Success Team (SST) referral

Tier 3: Individual Targeted Skill Interventions

- Tiers 1 and 2 strategies with frequency/length of intervention increased
- Tiers 1 and 2 strategies with group size decreased
- One-on-one with teacher and/or specialist
- Adapted content, methodology, and/or instructional delivery
- Parent involvement
- SST referral for possible Special Education (SPED) assessment

Note: Possible SPED placement

Source: Dr. Juvenal Luza, Slainas City Elementary School District, Salinas, CA.

Tool 5.6 Student Intervention Summary

Date _____ Follow-Up Date _____

Student Intervention Team Summary Form

Student Name _____ Grade _____ Birth Date _____

Teacher _____ Primary Language _____

Student Attendance _____ Standards-Based Assessment _____ Scale Scores: English Learner _____

Math _____ Migrant _____ Retained (if yes, when?) _____

Student History (medical, family, etc.)

Student Strengths

Concerns (Prioritize)

Brainstorm Strategies

Actions	Who	When

Team Members/Titles

Parent _____ Administrator _____ Classroom Teacher _____ Special Education Teacher _____

Speech Therapist _____ Psychologist _____ Intervention Specialist _____

Source: Dr. Juvenal Luza, Slainas City Elementary School District, Salinas, CA.

Tool 5.7   Academic/Behavior Pyramid

Academic Systems

Intensive Individual Interventions: 1–5%

- Individual students
- Assessment-based
- High intensity
- Of longer duration

Targeted Group Interventions: 5–10%

- Some students (at-risk)
- High efficiency
- Rapid response

Universal Interventions: 80–90%

- All students
- Preventative, proactive

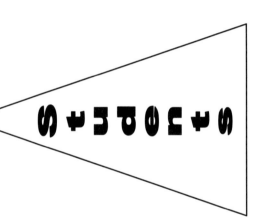

Behavioral Systems

Intensive Individual Interventions: 1–5%

- Individual students
- Assessment-based
- Intense, durable procedures

Targeted Group Interventions: 5–10%

- Some students (at-risk)
- High efficiency
- Rapid response

Universal Interventions: 80–90%

- All students
- Preventative, proactive

Tool 5.8   **Positive Behavior Support Observation Form**

Targeted Behavior: _____

Setting: _____

Antecedent: _____

Start Time: _____ End Time: _____

Baseline Data

Time/Latency	Frequency	Duration = Number of Seconds/ Minutes Before Complying to Multiple Prompts	Intensity Low = 1 High = 3	Topography

| Tool 5.9 | Student Observation of Behavior |

What did I do?

↓

What happened?

↓

What were my other choices?

↓

What will I do next time?

Tool 5.10	Behavior Progress Monitoring

Student Name: _____ Date: _____

Activity/ Subject/Time	Completed Assignment	Target Behavior 1	Target Behavior 2	Target Behavior 3	Extra Credit Points	Initials

Total Points _____

Above and Beyond = 35–40 points

Hit the Target = 20–35 points

Needs to Improve = <20 points

Teacher Comments _____

_____

_____

Parent Signature _____ Student Signature _____

| Tool 7.1 | Fifteen Skills for School and Work |

Discuss how these skills will be important in a school and work setting:

Skills	School Setting	Work Setting
1. Punctuality		
2. Following Directions		
3. Speaking Skills		
4. Written Skills		
5. Listening Skills		
6. Organization		
7. Note Taking		
8. Decision Making		
9. Problem Solving		
10. Teamwork		
11. Dependability		
12. Responsibility		
13. Planning		
14. Motivation		
15. Leadership		

Tool 7.2	Transition Checklist: Middle School to High School

This checklist of transition activities can assist the special education teacher when preparing transition plans with the student and Individualized Education Program team for a student's transition from middle school to high school. The student's skills and interests will determine which items on the checklist are relevant.

Student Transition Checklist

- ❏ Identify personal learning styles and the necessary accommodations to be a successful learner and worker.
- ❏ Identify career interests and skills, complete interest and career inventories, and identify additional education or training requirements.
- ❏ Explore options for college or other forms of postsecondary education.
- ❏ Learn to communicate your interests, preferences, and needs.
- ❏ Be able to explain your disability and the accommodations you need.
- ❏ Learn to communicate your interests, preferences, and needs.
- ❏ Look into assistive technology tools that can increase community involvement and employment opportunities.
- ❏ Broaden your experiences with community activities and expand your friendships.

| Tool 7.3 | Transition Checklist: High School to Graduation |

This checklist of transition activities can assist the special education teacher when preparing transition plans with the student and Individualized Education Program team for a student's transition from high school to graduation. The student's skills and interests will determine which items on the checklist are relevant.

Student Transition Checklist

❐ Develop an educational plan to align with your chosen career pathway.
❐ Identify options for future living arrangements.
❐ Identify community support services and programs (vocational rehabilitation, county services, centers for independent living, etc.).
❐ Invite adult service providers, peers, and others to the transition/Individualized Education Program meeting.
❐ Match career interests and skills with vocational course work and community work experience.
❐ Gather more information on postsecondary programs and the support services offered; make arrangements for accommodations to take college entrance exams (if appropriate).
❐ Begin a résumé and update it as needed.
❐ Begin building your job skills (e.g., look for summer or part-time employment).
❐ Annually update and adjust your educational plan to meet your needs.

Tool 7.4   Transition Checklist: High School to Postsecondary

This checklist of transition activities can assist the special education teacher when preparing transition plans with the student and Individualized Education Program team for a student's transition from high school to postsecondary life and activities. The student's skills and interests will determine which items on the checklist are relevant.

Student Transition Checklist

❏ Prepare for move from high school to college and/or employment, including scheduling, transportation, and other supports.

❏ Identify health care providers and become informed about sexuality and family-planning issues.

❏ Determine the need for financial support (supplemental Social Security income, state financial supplemental programs, Medicare).

❏ Learn and practice communication skills and social skills for different settings (employment, school, recreation, with peers).

❏ Explore guardianships.

❏ Practice independent living skills (e.g., budgeting, cooking, laundry).

❏ Identify needed personal assistance services, and, if appropriate, learn to direct and manage these services.

Tool 10.1	Teacher Reference Sheet of Family Background

Student's Name	Student's Parents' Names	Family's Ethnicity	Family's Home Language	Translator Required (Yes or No)?	Name and Contact Information of Cultural Expert or Community Representative (if Required)	Any Other Linguistic or Cultural Needs of Student or Student's Parents
1.						
2.						
3.						
4.						
5.						
6.						
7.						
8.						
9.						
10.						
11.						
12.						

Index

CORWIN
A SAGE Company

The Corwin logo—a raven striding across an open book—represents the union of courage and learning. Corwin is committed to improving education for all learners by publishing books and other professional development resources for those serving the field of PreK–12 education. By providing practical, hands-on materials, Corwin continues to carry out the promise of its motto: **"Helping Educators Do Their Work Better."**